The Law Commission
Consultation Paper No 156

DOUBLE JEOPARDY

A Consultation Paper

London: The Stationery Office

Applications for reproduction should be made in writing to
The Copyright Unit, Her Majesty's Stationery Office,
St. Clements House, 2–16 Colegate, Norwich, NR3 1BQ

ISBN 0 11 730241 4

Printed in the United Kingdom for The Stationery Office
J94197 10/99 C12 10170

THE LAW COMMISSION

DOUBLE JEOPARDY

CONTENTS

PART IV: THE SCOPE OF THE RULE AGAINST DOUBLE JEOPARDY

PART V: NEW EVIDENCE

PART VI: FUNDAMENTAL DEFECT IN THE FIRST TRIAL

ABBREVIATIONS

In this paper we use the following abbreviations:

Article 4: Article 4 of Protocol 7 to the European Convention on Human Rights

CPS: Crown Prosecution Service

ECHR: European Convention on Human Rights

ICCPR: International Covenant on Civil and Political Rights

the Macpherson report: The Stephen Lawrence Inquiry – Report of an Inquiry by Sir William Macpherson of Cluny (1999) Cm 4262

Strasbourg Commission: European Commission of Human Rights

Strasbourg Court: European Court of Human Rights

EUROPEAN COURT OF HUMAN RIGHTS CASES

The judgments of the European Court of Human Rights and the decisions and reports of the European Commission on Human Rights referred to in this consultation paper are reported in the following publications:

> The official publications of the ECHR, published by Carl Heysmanns Verlag. Up to 1996, judgments were published in Series A (Judgments and Decisions). Thereafter, they are published in yearly volumes as "Reports of Judgments and Decisions". The citations in this paper before 1996 are in the form *Gradinger v Austria* A 328-C (1995); that is Series A (Judgments and Decisions), volume 328, case C (ie the third case reported in that volume. If there is no letter, the volume contains a single judgment). After 1996, they are in the form *Oliveira v Switzerland* 1998-V p 1990; that is the 1998 volume of Reports of Judgments and Decisions, part V, at page 1990.

> The European Human Rights Reports, a series published by Sweet and Maxwell, which includes judgments of the Court and some Commission decisions. Cases are referred to in the form *Wingrove v UK* (1997) 24 EHRR 1 (volume 24 of the series, page 1).

> Decisions and Reports of the European Commission on Human Rights, published by the Council of Europe, and cited in the form *G v Federal Republic of Germany* (1989) 60 DR 252 (volume 60, page 252).

The date of unreported cases is given. Transcripts are obtainable on the European Court of Human Rights website (http://www.dhcour.coe.fr).

PART I
INTRODUCTION

1.1 On 2 July 1999 the Secretary of State for the Home Department made a reference to this Commission in the following terms:

> To consider the law of England and Wales relating to double jeopardy (after acquittal), taking into account: recommendation 38 of the Macpherson Report on the Stephen Lawrence Inquiry that consideration should be given to permit prosecution after acquittal where fresh and viable evidence is presented; the powers of the prosecution to re-instate criminal proceedings; and also the United Kingdom's international obligations; and to make recommendations.

1.2 We welcome this reference, as we are conscious of the tension between two basic principles affecting the fundamental rights of citizens. The first was stated by Blackstone as follows:

> The plea of autrefois acquit, or a former acquittal, is grounded on this universal maxim of the common law of England, that no man is to be brought into jeopardy of his life or limb more than once for the same offence … [T]he plea of autrefois convict, or a former conviction for the same identical crime … is a good plea in bar to an indictment. And this depends upon the same principle as the former, that no man ought to be twice brought in danger of his life for one and the same crime.[1]

1.3 A classic modern statement of this principle is that of Black J, in the Supreme Court of the United States:

> The underlying idea, one that is deeply ingrained in at least the Anglo-American system of jurisprudence, is that the State with all its resources and power should not be allowed to make repeated attempts to convict an individual for an alleged offence, thereby subjecting him to embarrassment, expense and ordeal and compelling him to live in a continuing state of anxiety and insecurity, as well as enhancing the possibility that even though innocent he may be found guilty.[2]

1.4 This rule is of ancient origin: it is found in Roman law, and in the common law since the 12th century.[3] But another basic objective of the criminal law is to ensure that the guilty are convicted. It would undermine public confidence in the criminal justice system if guilty people could avoid conviction and punishment.

---

[1] 4 Commentaries, pp 335-6.

[2] *Green v US* 355 US 184, 2 L ed 2nd p 199 at p 201.

[3] See Martin Friedland, *Double Jeopardy* (1969) p 6.

1

THE BACKGROUND TO THE REFERENCE

1.5   The reference from the Home Secretary arose from the report of the Stephen Lawrence Inquiry.[4] There was great public dissatisfaction about the way in which the police inquiry into the murder of Stephen Lawrence had been conducted, and the Home Secretary set up a Committee of Inquiry. In that case, a private prosecution had been brought unsuccessfully against youths who were accused of the murder. The prosecution failed because the judge ruled that the identification evidence of the prosecution's main witness was too unreliable to be admitted. One of the points considered in the inquiry was the impossibility of bringing a fresh prosecution against those who were allegedly responsible for Stephen Lawrence's death but had been acquitted of it.

1.6   The report explains:

> Both we and others ... have considered, in the context of this case, whether the law which absolutely protects those who have been acquitted from any further prosecution for the same or a closely allied offence should prevail. If, even at this late stage, fresh and viable evidence should emerge against any of the three suspects who were acquitted, they could not be tried again however strong the evidence might be. We simply indicate that perhaps in modern conditions such absolute protection may sometimes lead to injustice. Full and appropriate safeguards would be essential. Fresh trials after acquittal would be exceptional. But we indicate that at least the issue deserves debate and reconsideration perhaps by the Law Commission, or by Parliament.[5]

1.7   One of the recommendations was:

> That consideration should be given to the Court of Appeal being given power to permit prosecution after acquittal where fresh and viable evidence is presented.[6]

1.8   This recommendation – described as "[o]ne of the Macpherson report's most controversial recommendations"[7] – has provoked much interest. Lord Hooson, a distinguished barrister,[8] believes that "to change the law on this matter because of [the Lawrence case] would be a very dangerous step indeed".[9] Others disagree.[10]

---

[4]   The Stephen Lawrence Inquiry – Report of an Inquiry by Sir William Macpherson of Cluny (1999) Cm 4262, referred to in this paper as the Macpherson report.

[5]   Para 7.46.

[6]   Recommendation 38. The inquiry's terms of reference required it "to identify the lessons to be learned for the investigation and prosecution of racially motivated crimes", but our understanding is that this recommendation was not intended to be confined to such crimes. In any event, we see no reason at present for the rules on double jeopardy to be different in the case of racist crime from those applicable to other kinds of crime.

[7]   *The Sunday Telegraph* 28 February 1999.

[8]   A Queen's Counsel and former leader of the Wales and Chester Circuit.

[9]   *Hansard* (HL) 24 February 1999, vol 597, col 1172.

[10]   See, eg, Sir Louis Blom-Cooper QC, *The Times* 21 September 1999.

We note also that other countries, including Germany, Denmark and Finland, allow a prosecution to be reopened in some circumstances where there is new evidence.[11]

THE IMPLICATIONS OF HUMAN RIGHTS LAW

1.9 We have considered the implications for English law of the United Nations' International Convention on Civil and Political Rights (ICCPR) and the European Convention on Human Rights (ECHR).[12] We attach great importance to Article 4(1)[13] of the Seventh Protocol to the Convention, which prohibits the bringing of a second prosecution for the same offence, but note that Article 4(2) permits the original proceedings to be reopened in certain circumstances. The UK has not yet ratified this Protocol, but the Government has indicated its intention to do so.[14]

1.10 When the Protocol has been signed, and the Human Rights Act 1998 comes into force on 2 October 2000, rights under Article 4 of the Protocol will become Convention rights.[15] In consequence, the English courts will have to take account, in construing and enforcing these rights, of the decisions of the ECHR and opinions of the Commission to which we refer in detail in this paper. For the purposes of this paper we have disregarded the fact that the Seventh Protocol has not yet been ratified, and the fact that the Human Rights Act is not yet in force.

1.11 For the purpose of identifying the implications of these developments, we have sometimes found it convenient to draw a distinction in this paper between the law of the Convention on one hand and "English law" on the other. Strictly speaking this is inaccurate, because, once the Human Rights Act is in force, the law of the Convention will be *part* of English law. When we contrast the two, our references to "English law" should be understood as referring to the law of England and Wales *before* the law of the Convention is incorporated into it.

THE SCOPE OF THIS PAPER

1.12 In particular, we have found that the law of the Convention distinguishes three different ways in which the prosecution may seek to challenge an acquittal. The prosecution may

   (1) have rights of appeal;

   (2) seek to have the original proceedings *reopened* even after all avenues of appeal have been exhausted, or the time limit for an appeal has expired; or

   (3) seek to bring *new* proceedings, as distinct from reopening the old.

---

[11] Appendix B summarises the law in these and certain other foreign jurisdictions.

[12] See Part III below.

[13] See Appendix A below.

[14] Written Answer, *Hansard* (HL) 4 March 1999, vol 597, col 201.

[15] Human Rights Act 1998, s 1. An order under s 1(4) will be required for this purpose.

1.13 Of these three courses, the Convention permits the first, and in certain circumstances the second, but prohibits the third.[16] This prohibition is known in other countries as the principle of *ne bis in idem*.[17] English law does not draw such a clear distinction between the three kinds of challenge (especially the second and third), and the expression "double jeopardy" may refer to the first and second as well as the third. But both the recommendation in the Macpherson report and our terms of reference are framed in terms of *prosecution* after acquittal, which we interpret as including only the second and third. As regards rights of appeal, therefore, we confine ourselves to describing the existing law[18] and briefly mentioning the possibility of change,[19] and do not attempt to analyse the issues involved.

1.14 Both "double jeopardy" and *ne bis in idem* also include the case in which the proposed defendant has previously been *convicted* on the basis of the facts now alleged. Our reference is confined to double jeopardy following acquittal, and our primary focus is on acquittals rather than convictions; but many of the issues arise equally in both cases, and it would seem anomalous to make proposals only in respect of the former. Most of our proposals therefore apply to both, and in this respect this paper is wider in scope than either recommendation 38 of the Macpherson report or our terms of reference.

1.15 As we explain in Part II, in the English law of double jeopardy (in its widest sense) there are at present several different principles at work. The prosecution has certain, very limited, rights of appeal. Subject to certain exceptions, there is an absolute rule against charging a defendant with the same offence twice. In the case of trial on indictment this rule takes the form of a special plea, called "autrefois acquit" where the defendant has previously been acquitted of the offence charged and "autrefois convict" where he or she has previously been convicted of it. In this paper we refer collectively to these two rules (as well as the corresponding rule in relation to summary trial) as "the autrefois rule". The rule against double jeopardy after an acquittal is subject to a statutory exception where the acquittal is shown to have been "tainted" by interference with, or intimidation of, jurors or witnesses.

1.16 In addition, there is a discretion to stay proceedings which would be an abuse of the process of the court, which includes the situation where it is unfair that the defendant should be prosecuted at all; and, in the absence of special circumstances, the court has a duty to stay a prosecution which, though for a different offence, is based on the same or substantially the same facts as a previous acquittal or conviction of the same defendant. Another safeguard is the rule in

---

[16] At least where the new proceedings are for *the same offence* as the old, and arguably also where they are for a different offence but are based on the same facts. See paras 3.19 – 3.27 below.

[17] A person may not be prosecuted twice for the same thing.

[18] See paras 2.11 – 2.13 below.

[19] See Part XI below.

Sambasivam,[20] which prevents the prosecution from asserting that the defendant was in fact guilty of an offence of which he or she has previously been acquitted.

THE STRUCTURE OF THIS PAPER

1.17 In Part II we provide an outline of the present law. In Part III we examine the relevant provisions of the ICCPR and the ECHR, and in particular Article 4 of Protocol 7,[21] which (in the light of the Human Rights Act) makes it necessary that the law of England and Wales should continue to include a rule against double jeopardy. In Part IV we examine the justifications for such a rule, and conclude that they justify not only retaining the autrefois rule but extending it beyond its present scope. In Parts V and VI we discuss possible exceptions to the rule in two cases where this is permitted by Article 4(2) – namely where new evidence is discovered, and where there was a fundamental defect in the first trial.

1.18 In Part VII we consider what role should be played in the new regime by the existing judicial discretions to prevent proceedings which are unfair. In Part VIII we examine the rule in *Sambasivam*, that the prosecution may not challenge a previous acquittal. In Part IX we discuss the circumstances in which a person should and should not be regarded as having been acquitted or convicted for the purpose of the rule against double jeopardy and (if it is retained) the rule in *Sambasivam*. In Part X we consider whether the changes we provisionally propose should have retrospective effect. In Part XI we raise the possibility of extending the prosecution's rights of appeal. Part XII is a list of our provisional proposals, and other issues on which we invite views.

SUMMARY OF MAIN PROPOSALS

1.19 Our main provisional proposals are as follows.

(1) Subject to certain exceptions, the rule against double jeopardy should be retained.

(2) The rule should be extended, so as to apply not only

   (a) (as at present) where the prosecution seeks a conviction for an offence which is in law the same as one of which the defendant has previously been acquitted or convicted, but also

   (b) where it seeks a conviction for a different offence based on the same or substantially the same facts as a previous charge on which the defendant was acquitted or convicted.[22]

(3) It should be possible for the High Court to quash an acquittal on the grounds of new evidence[23] – but only where

---

[20] *Sambasivam v Public Prosecutor, Federation of Malaya* [1950] AC 458.

[21] In this paper we refer to Article 4 of Protocol 7 simply as "Article 4".

[22] Para 4.16 below.

[23] Para 5.17 below.

(a) if the defendant were convicted of the offence now alleged, the sentence would probably be of a specified minimum severity;[24]

(b) the new evidence makes the prosecution's case substantially stronger than it was at the first trial;[25]

(c) there is a very high probability of the defendant being convicted at a retrial;[26]

(d) the defendant has not previously been acquitted of the offence at a trial held by virtue of this exception to the double jeopardy rule;[27]

(e) the new evidence could not, with due diligence, have been adduced at the first trial;[28] and

(f) the court is satisfied that, in all the circumstances of the case, it is in the interests of justice to quash the acquittal.[29]

(4) The tainted acquittal procedure should be extended so that it applies where the administration of justice offence involves interference with or intimidation of a judge or a magistrate.[30] We invite views on whether, and if so in what circumstances, it should be sufficient to show that an administration of justice offence was *committed*, without the need for anyone to be *convicted* of it.[31] The procedure should be reformed so as to comply with Article 6 of the ECHR.[32]

(5) Subject to the rule against double jeopardy and the rules against the admission of prejudicial evidence, the prosecution should not be precluded from challenging an acquittal in any subsequent criminal proceedings against the same defendant.[33]

1.20 We are grateful for the assistance that we have received in preparing this paper from our consultant, Mr Ben Emmerson of Doughty Street Chambers.

---

[24] Para 5.27 below. We invite views on what that specified minimum should be, but express a provisional preference for three years' imprisonment: para 5.29 below.

[25] Para 5.38 below.

[26] Para 5.42 below.

[27] Para 5.60 below.

[28] Para 5.48 below.

[29] Para 5.51 below.

[30] Para 6.8 below.

[31] Para 6.12 below.

[32] Para 6.40 below.

[33] Para 8.40 below.

PART II
THE PRESENT LAW OF DOUBLE JEOPARDY

2.1 In this part we describe the two ways in which English law currently protects a defendant against double jeopardy. First is the basic rule that, following a valid conviction or acquittal, a defendant cannot be subjected again to trial for the same offence ("*the autrefois rule*"). We discuss three exceptions, or apparent exceptions, to this rule.

2.2 Secondly, there is a discretion to stay proceedings which would be an abuse of the process of the court because it is unfair that the defendant should be prosecuted; and, in the absence of special circumstances, the court is *required* to stay proceedings where the defendant has already been acquitted or convicted (albeit of a different offence) on the same or substantially the same facts ("*the Connelly principle*").

THE AUTREFOIS RULE

2.3 The doctrines of autrefois acquit and autrefois convict state that no-one may be put in peril twice for the same offence. Accordingly, if the accused has previously been acquitted or convicted (or could, by an alternative verdict, have been convicted) of the same offence as that with which he or she is now charged, a plea of autrefois will bar the prosecution.

Identity in law and fact

2.4 The offence with which the defendant is now charged must be identical to the offence of which he or she was previously acquitted or convicted. Thus in *Connelly v DPP*[1] the rule was held not to protect the defendant from being tried for robbery after being acquitted of a murder committed in the course of the robbery.[2] Lord Devlin explained:

> The word "offence" embraces both the facts which constitute the crime and the legal characteristics which make it an offence. For the doctrine to apply it must be the same offence both in fact and in law.[3]

2.5 This narrow view of the rule was confirmed recently by the Court of Appeal in *Beedie*,[4] holding that in *Connelly* the majority had "identified a narrow principle of

---

[1] [1964] AC 1254.

[2] The Court of Appeal had directed a verdict of acquittal, having allowed an appeal against the defendant's conviction for murder.

[3] *Connelly v DPP* [1964] AC 1254, 1339–1340. Lord Reid (at p 1295) and Lord Pearce (at p 1368) agreed. The alternative view that the principle applied also where the offences were substantially the same ([1964] AC 1254 at p 1305, *per* Lord Morris of Borth-y-Gest) was not adopted by the majority. Lord Morris's speech includes a detailed review of the English authorities over 400 years.

[4] [1998] QB 356, 361, *per* Rose LJ.

autrefois, applicable only where the same offence is alleged in the second indictment".[5] The rule therefore did not apply where the defendant, having already pleaded guilty to summary offences under the Health and Safety at Work Act 1974 on the basis of his failure to maintain a gas fire in residential premises owned by him, was charged with the manslaughter of a resident who died from carbon monoxide poisoning as a result.[6]

2.6   Even on this narrow view, however, it is only in *law* that the offence charged must be identical to the previous charge. The *facts* need only be *substantially* the same. As Lord Devlin put it, "I have no difficulty about the idea that one set of facts may be substantially but not exactly the same as another", whereas, in respect of identity in law, "legal characteristics are precise things and are either the same or not".[7]

The need for a valid acquittal or conviction

2.7   For a plea of autrefois to succeed there must previously have been a *valid* acquittal or conviction. This means, first, that the defendant must have been acquitted or convicted by a court of competent jurisdiction[8] and the proceedings must not have been ultra vires.[9] Thus a purported acquittal by a magistrates' court of an offence triable only on indictment will not found a plea of autrefois acquit.[10] Second, a purported acquittal or conviction by a competent court does not preclude a subsequent prosecution if the proceedings were so irregular as to be a nullity – for example, where magistrates purported to acquit without giving the prosecution an opportunity to adduce evidence,[11] or where two defendants were tried together without being joined in the same indictment.[12] An invalid acquittal cannot found a plea of autrefois because in law it does not exist. It is for this reason also that the Court of Appeal cannot "quash" an invalid conviction. However, it can order the

---

[5]   [1998] QB 356, 360.

[6]   But it was held that the second prosecution should have been stayed as an abuse of process: see para 2.22 below.

[7]   [1964] AC 1254, 1340. Lord Morris' view, that the new charge need only be *substantially* the same as the earlier one, is reflected in the statutory provisions applying the principle of double jeopardy to military law. For example, the Army Act 1955, s 134(1), as amended by the Armed Forces Act 1991, provides that in certain circumstances a person "shall not be liable in respect of the same or substantially the same offence to be tried by court-martial". The amendment predates *Beedie* [1998] QB 356, where Lord Devlin's analysis was preferred.

[8]   This requirement is satisfied if the court concerned was a *foreign* court of competent jurisdiction: *Treacy v DPP* [1971] AC 537, 562.

[9]   *R v Kent JJ, ex p Machin* [1952] 2 QB 355. The Divisional Court quashed M's conviction and committal for sentence for the offences of larceny and obtaining credit by fraud because the correct procedure for determining mode of trial had not been complied with and so the magistrates had acted ultra vires. Lord Goddard CJ at p 361 expressed the hope that there would be no further proceedings, but said that the prosecution was entitled to recharge M as he had "never been technically in peril".

[10]   *West* [1964] 1 QB 15.

[11]   *R v Dorking JJ, ex p Harrington* [1984] 1 AC 743.

[12]   *Crane v DPP* [1921] 2 AC 299.

conviction to be "set aside and annulled",[13] and award a "venire de novo" (a new trial, as distinct from a retrial after a valid trial).[14]

2.8   The need for an acquittal or conviction at the end of the first trial means that the autrefois rule does not apply where the defendant is discharged in committal proceedings,[15] where a summons is withdrawn before the defendant has pleaded to it,[16] where the information is dismissed owing to the non-appearance of the prosecutor,[17] or where the information was so faulty that the accused could never have been in jeopardy on it.[18] In these cases, there is no finding of the court which amounts to an acquittal.

2.9   Conversely, if the trial is validly commenced and ends in an unequivocal verdict by a properly constituted tribunal, the fact that there was irregularity in the proceedings does not invalidate the verdict, and a retrial is possible only if ordered under the statutory powers of an appellate court.[19]

Exceptions to the autrefois rule

2.10   Under the present law, there are three circumstances in which an apparently valid conviction or acquittal may be followed by a further trial for the same offence: *prosecution appeal*, *retrial following appeal against conviction*, and *tainted acquittals*.

Prosecution appeals

2.11   In general the prosecution has no right of appeal against an acquittal; but there are two exceptions to this rule.

CASE STATED

2.12   First, in the case of a *summary* acquittal, the prosecution may appeal to the Divisional Court on the ground that the decision "is wrong in law or is in excess of jurisdiction".[20] If the appeal succeeds, the Divisional Court can substitute a conviction for the acquittal and sentence the respondent, remit the case to the magistrates with a direction to convict and proceed to sentence, or (if a fair trial would still be possible) order a rehearing before the same or a different bench.[21] There is a similar right of appeal to the Divisional Court where the Crown Court allows an appeal against summary conviction.[22]

---

[13] *R v Booth, Wood and Molland* [1999] Crim LR 413.

[14] *Crane v DPP* [1921] 2 AC 299.

[15] *R v Manchester City Magistrates, ex p Snelson* [1977] 1 WLR 911.

[16] *R v Grays JJ, ex p Low* [1990] QB 54, especially at p 59, *per* Nolan J.

[17] *R v Bennett and Bond, ex p Bennet* (1908) 72 JP 362.

[18] *Dabhade* [1993] QB 329.

[19] *Rose* [1982] AC 822.

[20] Magistrates' Courts Act 1980, s 111(1); Supreme Court Act 1981, s 28(1).

[21] Supreme Court Act 1981, s 28A as inserted by the Statute Law (Repeals) Act 1993, s 1(2), Sched 2, part 1, para 9; *Griffith v Jenkins* [1992] 2 AC 76.

[22] Magistrates' Courts Act 1980, s 28.

2.13 Where the Criminal Division of the Court of Appeal quashes a conviction, the prosecution can appeal to the House of Lords only if the Court of Appeal certifies that its decision involves a point of law of general public importance *and* either the Court of Appeal or the House of Lords gives leave.[23] The position is similar (with the substitution of the Divisional Court for the Court of Appeal) where the conviction is quashed by the Divisional Court of the Queen's Bench Division of the High Court on an appeal by case stated.[24] The House of Lords can order the magistrates to retry the case.[25]

Retrial following appeal against conviction

2.14 When *Connelly* was decided, there was no provision for retrial following appeal against conviction. As Lord Reid explained, "Refusal to allow a new trial has always been put on the ground of fairness to the accused".[26] However, a limited power to order retrial was introduced in 1964[27] and later extended. The Court of Appeal now has power to order a retrial whenever it allows an appeal against conviction, provided that "the interests of justice so require".[28]

Tainted acquittals

2.15 The Criminal Procedure and Investigations Act 1996 provided for the first time a procedure by which a person could be retried for an offence of which he or she had already been acquitted, if the acquittal was "tainted".[29] This procedure is available where

(a) a person has been acquitted of an offence, and

(b) a person has been convicted of an administration of justice offence[30] involving interference with or intimidation of a juror or a witness (or potential witness) in any proceedings which led to the acquittal.[31]

---

[23] Criminal Appeal Act 1968, s 33.

[24] Administration of Justice Act 1960, ss1(1)(a) and 2(1).

[25] Administration of Justice Act 1960, s1(4).

[26] [1964] AC 1254, 1295.

[27] Criminal Appeal Act 1964, s 1(1).

[28] Criminal Appeal Act 1968, s 7. There are limits on the offences for which the defendant may be retried. If he or she is convicted, the sentence must not be of greater severity than that passed following the original trial: s 8(4), Sched 2, para 2(1).

[29] Criminal Procedure and Investigations Act 1996, ss 54–57.

[30] This means the offence of perverting the course of justice, the offence under the Criminal Justice and Public Order Act 1994, s 51(1) (intimidation etc of witnesses, juries and others) or an offence of aiding, abetting, counselling, procuring, suborning or inciting another person to commit an offence under the Perjury Act 1911, s 1: Criminal Procedure and Investigations Act 1996, s 54(6).

[31] Criminal Procedure and Investigations Act 1996, s 54(1).

2.16   If these conditions are met, and it appears to the court before which the person was convicted that there is a real possibility that, but for the interference or intimidation, the acquitted person would not have been acquitted, and that it would not be contrary to the interests of justice to take proceedings against the acquitted person for the offence of which he or she was acquitted, and the court certifies that this is so, an application may be made to the High Court for an order quashing the acquittal.[32]

2.17   The High Court may then make an order under section 54(3) of the Act quashing the acquittal, but only if

(1)   it appears to the High Court likely that, but for the interference or intimidation, the acquitted person would not have been acquitted;

(2)   it does not appear to the court that, because of lapse of time or for any other reason, it would be contrary to the interests of justice to take proceedings against the acquitted person for the offence of which he or she was acquitted;

(3)   it appears to the court that the acquitted person has been given a reasonable opportunity to make written representations to the court; and

(4)   it appears to the court that the conviction for the administration of justice offence will stand.

2.18   Where the High Court quashes the acquittal under section 54(3), new proceedings may be taken against the acquitted person for the offence of which he or she was acquitted.[33]

ABUSE OF PROCESS

2.19   The House of Lords' decision in *Connelly*[34] established that, outside the boundaries of the strict autrefois rule, protection against double jeopardy is provided by a special application of the abuse of process rules. The principle of abuse of process as it is now understood covers both cases in which it is not possible for the defendant to receive a fair trial, and cases in which, although the defendant could be fairly tried, it is unfair to put him or her on trial.[35] In the first category are cases in which there has been a delay between the commission of the offence and the trial, where potential evidence has been lost or destroyed,[36] or

---

[32]   *Ibid*, s 54(2), (3) and (5).

[33]   *Ibid*, s 54(4).

[34]   [1964] AC 1254.

[35]   See the distinction drawn in *Beckford* [1996] 1 Cr App R 94.

[36]   *McNamara and McNamara* [1998] Crim LR 278.

there has been prejudicial pre-trial publicity.[37] The second category includes cases in which the prosecution has gone back on promises not to prosecute or to discontinue proceedings,[38] and where the defendant has been brought within the jurisdiction in unlawful or unconscionable ways.[39]

2.20   It remains rare for a case to be stayed. The formal burden of proof (on the balance of probabilities)[40] rests on the defendant, who normally has to show that there is "something so unfair and wrong that the court should not allow a prosecutor to proceed with what is in all other respects a regular proceeding".[41]

The *Connelly* principle

2.21   Under the *Connelly* principle this burden is reversed. As Lord Devlin explained, where a person has once been tried in respect of particular facts, it is prima facie oppressive to put him or her on trial a second time in relation to those same facts, because it will normally be the case that the second charge could and should have been dealt with at the same time as the first. He went on:

> As a general rule a judge should stay an indictment (that is, order that it remain on the file not to be proceeded with) when he is satisfied that the charges therein are founded on the same facts as the charges in a previous indictment on which the accused has been tried, or form or are a part of a series of offences of the same or a similar character as the offences charged in the previous indictment. He will do this because as a general rule it is oppressive to an accused for the prosecution not to use rule 3[42] where it can properly be used. But a second trial on the same or similar facts is not always and necessarily oppressive, and there may in a particular case be special circumstances which make it just and convenient in that case.[43]

2.22   The importance of this principle as a protection against double jeopardy was confirmed by the Court of Appeal in *Beedie*.[44] It was held that, while the autrefois

---

[37]   *Reade* unreported, 15 October 1993.

[38]   *Bloomfield* [1997] 1 Cr App R 135; *Townsend, Dearsley and Bretscher* [1997] 2 Cr App R 540.

[39]   *R v Horseferry Road Magistrates' Court, ex p Bennett* [1994] 1 AC 42; *Mullen v Conoco Ltd* [1998] QB 382.

[40]   *R v Crown Court at Norwich, ex p Belsham* (1992) 94 Cr App R 382; *Gin (George Tan Soon) v Cameron* [1992] 2 AC 205, PC; but see *R v Telford JJ, ex p Badhan* [1991] 2 QB 78.

[41]   *Hui Chi-Ming* [1992] 1 AC 34, 57.

[42]   Indictments Act 1915, Sched 1, rule 3, which permitted a series of offences of the same or a similar character to be joined in the same indictment. See now rule 9 of the Indictment Rules 1971 (SI 1971 No 1253). (Footnote supplied)

[43]   [1964] AC 1254, 1359–1360. As stated by Lord Devlin, the principle is wide enough to catch a subsequent prosecution for an offence which, though based on different facts from that charged in the first indictment, could and should have been included in that indictment on the basis that the two offences form "a series of offences of the same or a similar character". For example, it would apply to an indictment charging a burglary in July which could have been combined with one charging a similar burglary in June. Even if the rule is really this wide (which seems doubtful) this sort of case is not an example of double jeopardy, and we do not deal with it in this paper.

[44]   [1998] QB 356.

rule did not protect against subsequent prosecution for a different offence on the same facts, the defendant in such a case is instead protected by a presumption that the proceedings should be stayed in the absence of special circumstances to justify them.[45]

Special circumstances

2.23 The authorities provide little guidance as to what might constitute "special circumstances" sufficient to justify a new charge on the same facts. In *Connelly* itself, Lord Devlin declined to attempt "a comprehensive definition", but gave as an example a case where the prosecution considers that two charges should be charged separately, and prefers two indictments accordingly.

> In many cases this may be to the advantage of the defence. If the defence accepts the choice without complaint and avails itself of any advantage that may flow from it, I should regard that as a special circumstance ...[46]

This suggests a relatively narrow application for the rule, applicable to cases where the defence has in effect acquiesced in the separation of the trials.

2.24 A more useful example is provided by the recent decision of three former judges of the Court of Appeal,[47] sitting as the Court of Appeal for Gibraltar, in *Attorney General for Gibraltar v Leoni*.[48] The defendants were seen jettisoning cargo from their boat on the approach of a police launch. The police suspected that the cargo was cannabis, but could not prove this until the cargo was recovered; and by that time the defendants had already pleaded guilty to an offence of jettisoning cargo. The Court of Appeal held that this was not enough to bring the *Connelly* principle into play, because the charges of possessing and importing cannabis did not arise out of the same facts as the charges of jettisoning cargo. But the court went on to express the view that the recovery of the cannabis, after the defendants had been dealt with on the jettisoning charge, would in any event have amounted to special circumstances. It has long been established that the occurrence of some new *event* after a conviction for a lesser offence is no bar to a later prosecution for an aggravated offence: for instance, a defendant convicted of an assault can be prosecuted for manslaughter if the victim of the assault dies after the conviction.[49] The court drew an analogy between the occurrence of a new event and the discovery of new evidence.

---

[45] This casts doubt on the Divisional Court's dictum in *R v Forest of Dean JJ, ex p Farley* [1990] Crim LR 568, that there is a discretion to stay proceedings if to proceed after conviction or acquittal on a lesser charge would be oppressive or prejudicial, but that this will rarely be appropriate.

[46] [1964] AC 1254, 1360. He noted that, if the defence wished for a single trial of the two indictments, it could apply for an order in the form made in *Smith* [1958] 1 All ER 475.

[47] Sir Brian Neill (President), Sir John Waite JA and Sir Iain Glidewell JA, who gave the judgment of the court.

[48] Criminal Appeal No 4 of 1998, judgment given 19 March 1999; unreported.

[49] See para 2.27 below.

2.25   This supports the view that the discovery of new evidence may amount to a special circumstance for the purposes of the *Connelly* principle. It is noteworthy that the court took this view although the prosecution had been aware, at the time when the jettisoning charges were dealt with, that evidence of cannabis offences might yet be discovered. The argument for treating the discovery of new evidence as special circumstances must be all the stronger where, at the time of the first trial, the prosecution has no reason to suppose that evidence of another offence might become available.

The *Elrington* principle

2.26   In *Beedie*[50] the defence also relied on a further principle, derived from the old case of *Elrington*.[51] In that case, justices had dismissed an information for assault against the defendant. He was then indicted for causing grievous bodily harm, on the basis of the same assault. Cockburn CJ stated as a principle of general application that "whether a party accused of a minor offence is acquitted or convicted, he shall not be charged again on the same facts in a more aggravated form".[52] In *Beedie* the Court of Appeal treated this principle (as well as the wider principle stated by Lord Devlin in *Connelly*) as a factor relevant to the judge's decision whether to stay the proceedings.[53] On this view, the *Elrington* principle has the effect that the presumption in favour of a stay is *even stronger* where the second charge does not merely arise out of the same facts but is an aggravated form of the first.[54]

2.27   In any event, it is established that a person who has been convicted of an offence can be prosecuted for an aggravated form of the same offence if the facts constituting the aggravated offence were not in existence at the time of the conviction. Thus a person convicted of an assault can be charged with murder or manslaughter if the victim subsequently dies from the injuries sustained.[55] This is an exception to the *Elrington* principle.

---

[50]   [1998] QB 356; see para 2.22 above.

[51]   (1861) 1 B & S 688; 121 ER 170.

[52]   (1861) 1 B & S 688, 696.

[53]   [1998] QB 356, 366E–F.

[54]   Defence counsel cited *R v Forest of Dean JJ, ex p Farley* [1990] RTR 228, where Neill LJ at p 239 referred to the "*almost invariable* rule that where a person is tried on a lesser offence he is not to be tried again on the same facts for a more serious offence" (italics supplied).

[55]   *De Salvi* (1857) 10 Cox CC 481; *Thomas* [1950] 1 KB 26.

PART III
THE SIGNIFICANCE OF HUMAN RIGHTS LAW

3.1 In this part we discuss the implications for the English law of double jeopardy of the United Nations' International Covenant on Civil and Political Rights (ICCPR) and the European Convention on Human Rights (ECHR). We explain that Article 4(1) of Protocol 7 to the Convention prohibits the bringing of a second prosecution for the same offence, but that Article 4(2) permits the original proceedings to be reopened in certain circumstances. We then compare the requirements of the ECHR with the English law of double jeopardy. We conclude that English law is generally compliant with the ECHR, and indeed is for the most part less permissive of double jeopardy than the ECHR allows. In one respect, however, English law allows double jeopardy to occur in circumstances where the ECHR arguably does not.

THE BACKGROUND

3.2 The United Kingdom is bound under international law to ensure that its domestic practice complies with the obligations which it has undertaken under the ECHR[1] and the ICCPR.[2] Both treaties contain provisions which have a direct bearing on the issues considered in this consultation paper. The United Kingdom's international law obligations alone afford a sufficient basis for ensuring that any proposals for reform are compatible with the rights guaranteed under these important human rights treaties.

3.3 However, the ECHR will shortly enjoy an enhanced status in our national courts. The enactment of the Human Rights Act in November 1998 signalled Parliament's intention to give further effect in domestic law to the rights contained in the ECHR and to the rights contained in those protocols to the ECHR that the United Kingdom has ratified. The Home Secretary has announced that the substantive provisions of the 1998 Act will come into force in

---

[1] Article 1 of the ECHR provides: "The High Contracting Parties shall secure to everyone within their jurisdiction the rights and freedoms defined in Section I of this Convention". Article 13 provides: "Everyone whose rights and freedoms as set forth in this Convention are violated shall have an effective remedy before a national authority notwithstanding that the violation has been committed by persons acting in an official capacity".

[2] Article 2 of the ICCPR, as far as relevant, provides: "2(1) Each State Party to the present Covenant undertakes to respect and to ensure to all individuals within its territory and subject to its jurisdiction the rights recognized in the present Covenant, without distinction of any kind…; 2(2) Where not already provided for by existing legislative or other measures, each State Party to the present Covenant undertakes to take the necessary steps, in accordance with its constitutional processes and with the provisions of the present Covenant, to adopt such legislative or other measures as may be necessary to give effect to the rights recognized in the present Covenant; 2(3) Each State Party to the present Covenant undertakes: a) To ensure that any person whose rights or freedoms as herein recognized are violated shall have an effective remedy, notwithstanding that the violation has been committed by persons acting in an official capacity …".

October 2000. The Act will operate retrospectively in relation to criminal cases, without limit of time.[3]

3.4 There are three provisions of the ECHR which are relevant to the issues raised in this consultation paper: Article 6 (the right to a fair trial); Article 7 (the prohibition on retrospective application of the criminal law); and Article 4 of Protocol 7 (the prohibition on double jeopardy in criminal cases).[4] Articles 6 and 7 of the Convention are already binding on the United Kingdom, and are amongst the rights expressly incorporated by Schedule 1 to the Human Rights Act,[5] but the United Kingdom has not yet ratified Protocol 7.

3.5 Protocol 7 contains a number of specific rights relating to criminal proceedings, the expulsion of aliens, and equality between spouses. It was adopted so as to bring the ECHR into line with the broader range of rights protected under the ICCPR.[6] In its White Paper on the Human Rights Bill,[7] the Government expressed its intention to sign, ratify and incorporate[8] Protocol 7 once certain provisions of national law, unrelated to the issues under consideration in this consultation paper, have been amended. In the light of this commitment, we have decided to proceed on the assumption that the prohibition on double jeopardy embodied in Article 4 of the protocol will, in due course, be enforceable in the national courts, in accordance with the substantive provisions of the Human Rights Act.

THE APPROACH OF OTHER COUNCIL OF EUROPE MEMBER STATES

3.6 Before considering the United Kingdom's obligations under the ICCPR and the ECHR, we must refer briefly to the practice in other Council of Europe Member States, since this has had a significant influence on the scope of the double jeopardy prohibition under both treaties.

The concept of res judicata

3.7 All European states recognise the principle that once ordinary appellate remedies have been exhausted, or the relevant time limit for appealing has expired, a conviction or acquittal is to be regarded as irrevocable, and acquires the quality of res judicata.[9] The term "res judicata" is used in a number of different ways in different jurisdictions. In this paper we use it in the way in which it is used in the Explanatory Report to Protocol 7, and which informs the Convention case law. An acquittal or conviction is res judicata if it is final, in the sense that all *ordinary* procedures have been exhausted. In England, an acquittal in a trial on indictment is res judicata as soon as the jury deliver their verdict. Where provision is made for

---

[3] See Human Rights Act 1998, ss 22(4) and 7(1)(b).

[4] In this paper "Article 4" means Article 4 of Protocol 7 unless otherwise stated.

[5] Articles 6 and 7 are dealt with at paras 6.31 – 6.41 and 10.5 – 10.6 below.

[6] See Rights Brought Home: The Human Rights Bill (1997) Cm 3782, paras 4.9 and 4.14.

[7] *Ibid*, para 4.15.

[8] An order will be required under the Human Rights Act 1998, s 1(4).

[9] See Explanatory Report to Protocol 7 of the ECHR, CE Doc H (83) 3, para 22.

a prosecution right of appeal, an acquittal would become res judicata when either the time for appealing had elapsed, or an appeal had been determined. Similarly, a conviction in England is res judicata after the time limit for appealing has elapsed, or the Court of Appeal, Criminal Division (or, if a point of law is certified and leave is granted, the House of Lords) has determined the appeal.

3.8 For a determination to become res judicata, however, does not require that all *extraordinary*[10] remedies or procedures are exhausted. Thus in England, it is possible to challenge a conviction on indictment after it becomes res judicata by an appeal out of time to the Court of Appeal, Criminal Division, or by seeking a reference to the court from the Criminal Cases Review Commission. The distinction between ordinary procedures, which are available before the determination becomes res judicata, and extraordinary procedures available *after* that point, is important to an understanding of Article 4 of Protocol 7.

Reopening a final acquittal or conviction

3.9 Many states permit a final decision to be reopened if new evidence becomes available which demonstrates that the original verdict was wrong or if there has been a fundamental defect in the original proceedings. Provisions which permit the reopening of a final conviction or acquittal generally require the involvement of an appellate court. Where the original verdict is set aside in accordance with such a procedure the appellate court may, in some states, order a retrial. There is considerable variation between the practices adopted on this issue in the criminal procedure systems which make up the Council of Europe. In Italy, for example, once ordinary appellate remedies have been exhausted, a judgment becomes final and an acquitted or convicted person may not be tried again for the same offence, even if relevant new facts or evidence have become available.[11] In Finland, on the other hand, any criminal proceedings can be reopened if an acquittal has been obtained through fraud; and an acquittal of an offence punishable with two years' imprisonment can be reopened if new evidence becomes available which, had it been available at the trial, would in all probability have led to a conviction.[12]

3.10 Provisions permitting a final conviction or acquittal to be reopened are to be found in the criminal procedure systems of a number of Western European states.[13] In some states the rules apply in the same way whether the prosecution seeks to overturn a final acquittal or the defence seeks to overturn a final

---

[10] The distinction between ordinary and extraordinary procedures must depend on the actual practice of the state in question (or, possibly, on what is generally accepted in Council of Europe countries): it is not possible to derive any guidance from Article 4. But the criminal procedures of Council of Europe states are themselves governed by *other* parts of the Convention, particularly Article 6.

[11] See generally Christine Van den Wyngaert (ed) *Criminal Procedure Systems in the European Community* (1993) p 258.

[12] See Finland's Reservation to the ICCPR, Article 14, para 7, cited in Nowak, *CCPR Commentary* (1993) p 753.

[13] See generally Nowak, *CCPR Commentary* (1993) pp 272–273.

conviction. In other states, the right to apply to an appellate court to reopen a verdict which has the force of res judicata is available only to the defence.

THE INTERNATIONAL COVENANT ON CIVIL AND POLITICAL RIGHTS

3.11   The ICCPR was drafted by the United Nations Human Rights Commission in parallel with the drafting of the ECHR by the Council of Europe in the immediate aftermath of the Second World War. The two organisations worked closely together on the texts, and the Council of Europe relied in part on the drafts prepared by the Human Rights Commission.[14] However, the ICCPR was not finally adopted by the General Assembly of the United Nations until 1966, and did not enter into force until 1976. The rights contained in the ICCPR are broadly similar in their content to those contained in the ECHR, although there are a number of significant differences.

3.12   Article 14(7) of the ICCPR is as follows.

> No one shall be liable to be tried or punished again for an offence for which he has already been finally convicted or acquitted in accordance with the law and penal procedure of each country.

Article 14 applies both to the reopening of a conviction and to the reopening of an acquittal. Read literally, it therefore prohibits even the power of an appellate court to quash a criminal conviction and to order a retrial if new evidence or a procedural defect is discovered after the ordinary appeals process has been concluded. In its General Comment on Article 14(7),[15] however, the United Nations Human Rights Committee, the treaty body charged with implementing the ICCPR, expressed the view that the reopening of criminal proceedings "justified by exceptional circumstances" did not infringe the principle of double jeopardy. The Committee drew a distinction between the "resumption" of criminal proceedings, which it considered to be permitted by Article 14(7), and "retrial" which was expressly forbidden.

3.13   The distinction between "resumption" and "retrial" has not yet been expressly recognised in the law of England and Wales. It has, however, taken firm root in European human rights law, and is now reflected in Article 4(2) of Protocol 7 to the ECHR.

THE EUROPEAN CONVENTION ON HUMAN RIGHTS

3.14   When the ECHR was drafted in 1950, the original signatory States made no express reference to the prohibition on double jeopardy. In its early case law the Commission left open the question whether the principle could be implied into the right to a fair trial in Article 6.[16] In 1984, however, the Commission held that

---

[14]   The relationship between the ICCPR and the ECHR is explained in Cohen-Jonathon, *La Convention Européenne des Droits de L'Homme* (1989) at pp 15 ff.

[15]   General Comment 13/21, para 19.

[16]   See, for example, *X v Austria* (1970) 35 CD 151. The Convention institutions have, on occasion, implied into Article 6 guarantees which are absent from its text, but which are to

"the Convention guarantees neither expressly nor by implication the principle of *ne bis in idem*".[17] Shortly after this decision, on 22 November 1984, Protocol 7 to the ECHR was opened for signature. It entered into force, in respect of those states which had ratified it, on 1 November 1988.

3.15   Article 4 of Protocol 7 provides:

    (1)   No one shall be liable to be tried or punished again in criminal proceedings under the jurisdiction of the same State for an offence for which he has already been finally acquitted or convicted in accordance with the law and penal procedure of that State.

    (2)   The provisions of the preceding paragraph shall not prevent the reopening of the case in accordance with the law and penal procedure of the State concerned, if there is evidence of new or newly discovered facts, or if there has been a fundamental defect in the previous proceedings, which could affect the outcome of the case.

    (3)   No derogation from this Article shall be made under Article 15 of the Convention.

3.16   Article 4(1) thus embodies the principle of double jeopardy as it applies to the unilateral action of a prosecuting authority or private prosecutor. But Article 4(2) permits a case to be "reopened", in accordance with the provisions of domestic law, if there is "evidence of new or newly discovered facts", or if there has been "a fundamental defect in the previous proceedings".

The scope of Article 4(1)

Final acquittal or conviction

3.17   Article 4(1) prohibits the bringing of proceedings only where the defendant has been "finally acquitted or convicted" of the offence now charged, "in accordance with the law and penal procedure" of the state in question. The Explanatory Report to Protocol 7 states that a decision is to be regarded as final for the purposes of Article 4(1)

    if, according to the traditional expression, it has acquired the force of res judicata. This is the case when it is irrevocable, that is to say when no further ordinary remedies are available or when the parties have exhausted such remedies or have permitted the time limit to expire without availing themselves of them.

be found in analogous texts of the UN or other international organisations: *Funke v France* A 256-A (1993) (protection against self-incrimination as provided in Article 14(3)(g) of the ICCPR); *S v Switzerland* A 220 (1991) (confidentiality of privileged communications as provided in Article 8(2)(d) of the American Convention on Human Rights, and Article 93 of the Standard Minimum Rules for the Treatment of Prisoners); *V and T v UK* (Application No. 24888/94, 4 December 1998) (confidentiality of juvenile proceedings as provided in Article 40 of the UN Convention on the Rights of the Child, and the United Nations Standard Minimum Rules for the Administration of Juvenile Justice).

[17]   *S v Federal Republic of Germany* (1983) 39 DR 43.

Thus, for example, a defendant has not been "finally acquitted" if the acquittal is set aside, and a rehearing ordered, in the course of an ordinary appeal.

3.18 In theory, if the decision is not "final" until the expiry of the ordinary time-limits for appeal, there would be no breach where, immediately after an acquittal in a magistrates' court on a point of law, the prosecution brought fresh proceedings instead of exercising its right to appeal by case stated. That cannot be intended. In practice, the requirement of finality must be read as distinguishing between two different *kinds of proceeding* – namely fresh proceedings, on the one hand (at whatever stage after the acquittal or conviction), and an appeal against acquittal or sentence on the other.[18] Only the former is prohibited by Article 4.[19]

Prosecution for same offence

3.19 There are conflicting decisions as to whether Article 4(1) applies only where the second charge is in fact and law the same, or also to a second charge for a different offence based on the same facts.

3.20 The latter was the view taken in the first case in which the Strasbourg Court considered Article 4. This was *Gradinger v Austria*.[20] The applicant was convicted of a criminal offence of causing death by negligent driving, but acquitted of an aggravated form of the offence. This offence required proof that the amount of alcohol in his blood had exceeded the prescribed limit, and the court accepted medical evidence which placed his blood-alcohol level beneath that limit. The local administrative authorities subsequently acquired a medical report which contradicted the evidence adduced by the applicant at his trial. On the basis of the new report the authorities imposed on the applicant an administrative penalty (a fine) for driving with excess alcohol. The Strasbourg Court concluded that, following the acquittal in the first proceedings, Article 4(1) was applicable.[21] In determining whether Article 4(1) had been violated, the Court adopted a substantive rather than a formalistic approach to the double jeopardy principle. Although the elements of the two offences were different, and they pursued different aims, the blood-alcohol level required for the two offences was the same. Since both charges were "based on the same conduct" the Court concluded that there had been a violation of Article 4.

3.21 It is of interest that, although the case might be thought to have involved "new or newly discovered facts", there was no discussion in the judgment of the effect of

---

[18] There may be other routes to the same conclusion. It might be said, for example, that, by commencing fresh proceedings instead of appealing, the prosecution would have abandoned its right of appeal, thus rendering the acquittal "final"; or that the time limit for appealing would almost inevitably have expired (thus rendering the acquittal final) before the new proceedings were determined.

[19] But in certain circumstances it may be permissible under Article 4(2). See paras 3.28 – 3.31 below.

[20] A 328-C (1995).

[21] Although the second set of proceedings were classified as "administrative" for the purposes of national law, it was held that they fell to be categorised as criminal proceedings for the purpose of the Convention, applying the criteria laid down by the Court in *Engel v Netherlands (No. 1)* A 22 (1976) and *Öztürk v FRG* A 73 (1984).

Article 4(2), and there appears to have been no argument based on it. Presumably, this is because there was no relevant "law" or "penal procedure" providing for the "reopening" of the earlier proceedings in the particular circumstances.

3.22 By contrast, a narrow view of Article 4(1) was taken in the subsequent case of *Oliveira v Switzerland*.[22] The Court held that successive prosecutions will not violate Article 4 if they relate to separate offences arising out of the same act. The applicant was involved in a road traffic accident in which another motorist was seriously injured. Owing to an administrative error, her case was dealt with by the police magistrate, whose jurisdiction was limited to minor offences. The magistrate convicted her of a minor offence of failing to control her vehicle, and imposed a fine of 200 francs. He had no jurisdiction to consider the more serious offence of negligently inflicting physical injury, and he failed to refer the case to the district attorney as he was required to do under Swiss law. The district attorney's office subsequently issued a penal order fining the applicant 2,000 francs for the more serious offence. The conviction was upheld on appeal.

3.23 The applicant complained that she had been prosecuted twice in respect of the same offence. The Court rejected this complaint, holding that this was "a typical example of a single act constituting various offences". As the Court explained:

> The characteristic feature of this notion is that a single criminal act is split up into two separate offences, in this case the failure to control the vehicle and the negligent causing of physical injury. In such cases, the greater penalty will usually absorb the lesser one. There is nothing in that situation which infringes Article 4 of Protocol No 7 since that provision prohibits people being tried twice for the same offence, whereas in cases concerning a single act constituting various offences one criminal act constitutes two separate offences.[23]

3.24 The Court observed that it would have been more consistent with the principles governing the proper administration of justice for sentence in respect of both offences to have been passed by the same court in a single set of proceedings. Nevertheless, the fact that this had not occurred was irrelevant to the issues arising under Article 4 since

> that provision does not preclude separate offences, even if they are all part of a single criminal act, being tried by different courts, especially where, as in the present case, the penalties were not cumulative, the lesser being absorbed by the greater.[24]

3.25 In previous cases the Commission had consistently distinguished between successive prosecutions for the same offence, and prosecutions for multiple offences arising out of the same course of conduct.[25] But *Oliveira* goes further than

---

[22] 1998-V p 1990.

[23] *Ibid*, para 26.

[24] *Ibid*, para 27.

[25] In *Palaoro v Austria* (unreported, Application No 16718/90), for example, the Commission rejected as manifestly ill-founded a complaint brought under Article 4 by an applicant who

these cases, in that the second fine related to precisely the same act as the first. The only difference lay in the nature of the charges. The decision suggests that Article 4(1) is triggered only where the offence with which the defendant is charged is, *in law*, the same offence as that of which he or she was previously acquitted or convicted. This interpretation would mean that Article 4(1) went no further than the autrefois rule in English law.[26]

3.26 A point of distinction between the two cases might have been that in *Gradinger* the applicant had been *acquitted* of the aggravated offence, whereas in *Oliveira* the applicant had been *convicted* of the minor offence. The effect of the second set of proceedings in *Gradinger* was to call the previous acquittal into question; in *Oliveira* they had no such effect, but only exposed the applicant to a more severe penalty. But there is virtually no suggestion in the majority judgment that the distinction between a previous acquittal and a previous conviction was regarded as crucial.[27] Nor is there any support for it in the wording of Article 4(1) itself.

3.27 In *Oliveira* the Court itself considered that the analysis quoted above[28] was sufficient to distinguish *Gradinger*, noting that in that case two different courts had come to inconsistent findings on the applicant's blood-alcohol level. In a powerful dissenting judgment, Judge Repik disagreed:

> No difference can be seen between the Gradinger case and the Oliveira case that can justify these two wholly conflicting decisions. In both cases, the conduct that led to the prosecution was identical. In both cases, owing to a mistake by the court that first convicted the accused, one aspect of the actus was not taken into account in the conviction. Lastly, in both cases, the same conduct, aggravated by the aspect that the first court had omitted to take into account, led to a second conviction under a different legal qualification.

We prefer this view, and conclude that there is a real conflict between the two decisions.

---

had been convicted of two offences of exceeding the prescribed speed limit in the course of a single journey, since the two offences had been committed on separate sections of road. Similarly, in *Iskandarani v Sweden* (unreported, Application No 23222/94) the Commission rejected a complaint under Article 4 where the applicant had previously been convicted of abducting his daughter, and was subsequently prosecuted for withholding the child from her legal custodian after the abduction had occurred. These were separate offences arising out of the same course of criminal conduct, and Article 4 did not prohibit separate proceedings for such offences.

[26] See paras 2.3 – 2.5 above.

[27] Arguably there is a hint of this in the remark that successive prosecutions for different offences are permissible "especially where ... the penalties were not cumulative, the lesser being absorbed by the greater". But the word "especially" seems to imply that this consideration is not crucial. It is perhaps of interest that van Dijk and van Hoof's *Theory and Practice of the European Convention on Human Rights* (3rd ed 1998) says that in *Gradinger* the applicant was initially convicted, not mentioning the relevant acquittal of the aggravated offence. The authors can hardly have considered that the distinction between an acquittal and a conviction was of any moment. Van Dijk was one of the judges in *Gradinger*.

[28] Paras 3.23 – 3.24.

The scope of Article 4(2)

3.28 The reopening permitted by Article 4(2) must be distinguished from an appeal by the prosecution. A prosecution appeal is an ordinary procedure which may be invoked before the decision has become res judicata. Reopening is an extraordinary procedure which may be invoked *after* the decision is res judicata.

3.29 Although it is not specifically stated, we think it clear that Article 4(2) envisages a case being reopened only with the authority of a court. A simple decision by the prosecuting authorities to launch another prosecution is precluded altogether. This view is probably implicit in the reference to "reopening", as distinct from a fresh prosecution. In any event, it would in our view be contrary to the principle of the independence of the Court (guaranteed by Article 6 of the Convention) if the executive were permitted, of its own motion, to treat an earlier decision as of no effect.[29]

3.30 It follows that Article 4(2) does not create *exceptions* to the prohibition in Article 4(1): the two provisions are concerned with different kinds of proceeding. Article 4(1) prohibits the bringing of a second prosecution on the same facts. That prohibition is absolute, and is not affected by Article 4(2).

3.31 What Article 4(2) does is to permit a *different* way of challenging an acquittal, namely by persuading a higher court to "reopen" the original proceedings. Even this latter course of action is permitted only on certain specified grounds – namely that new evidence has been found, or that there was a fundamental defect in the original proceedings. In any other circumstances, the reopening of the case is prohibited; but this is the (implied) effect of Article 4(2), not Article 4(1).

ENGLISH LAW AND THE ECHR COMPARED

3.32 In this section we compare the English law of double jeopardy with the requirements of the ECHR. This involves asking two questions. First, in what circumstances (if any) is double jeopardy permitted by English law but not by the ECHR? And second, in what circumstances is it permitted by the ECHR but not by English law?

[29] In *Van der Hurk v Netherlands* A 288 (1994) the relevant legislation allowed the Minister to decide that a judgment of the Industrial Appeal Tribunal should not be implemented. The power had never been exercised and was due to be repealed. The Court found that the very existence of the power gave rise to a violation of Article 6, despite the fact that it had not been referred to in the proceedings, and "there was nothing to indicate that [it] had any influence on the way the tribunal handled and decided the cases which came before it" (para 47).

Similarly, in *Findlay v UK* 1997-I p 263, para 77, the Court concluded that the role of the "convening officer" who had the duty to confirm a decision of a court martial and to vary its sentence was "contrary to the well-established principle that the power to give a binding decision which may not be altered by a non-judicial authority is inherent in the very notion of 'tribunal' and can also be seen as a component of the 'independence' required by Article 6(1)".

Double jeopardy permitted by English law but not by the ECHR

3.33   We saw in Part II that, in English law, double jeopardy (or what might at first sight *appear* to be double jeopardy) is permitted in the following circumstances:

(1)   where the outcome of the first proceedings was not, and did not purport to be, an acquittal or a conviction;

(2)   where the outcome of the proceedings purported to be an acquittal or a conviction but was of no legal effect (for example, because the court lacked jurisdiction to try the offence charged) or is quashed by way of judicial review;

(3)   where a conviction is quashed on appeal, but the appellate court orders a retrial;

(4)   where an acquittal is quashed under sections 54 and 55 of the Criminal Procedure and Investigations Act 1996 (a tainted acquittal); and

(5)   where the offence charged, though based on the same facts as one of which the defendant has previously been acquitted or convicted, is not the same offence, and the presumption against allowing such proceedings is displaced by special circumstances.

We must consider whether, in each of these cases where double jeopardy is permissible under English law, it is also permissible under the ECHR.

No acquittal or conviction

3.34   There are a number of ways in which an English court's consideration of an alleged offence can end without the defendant being acquitted or convicted, with the result that he or she can be prosecuted again for the same offence. They appear to include the following:

(1)   the discharge of the jury, without a verdict being obtained from them;

(2)   the quashing of an indictment following a motion to quash;[30]

(3)   the discharge of the defendant at the conclusion of committal proceedings;[31]

(4)   the dismissal of an information on the non-appearance of the prosecutor;[32]

(5)   the dismissal of an information which is too faulty for the defendant to have been in jeopardy on it;[33]

(6)   the discontinuance of proceedings under section 23 or 23A of the Prosecution of Offences Act 1985;

---

[30]   *Newland* [1988] QB 402.

[31]   *R v Manchester City Stipendiary Magistrate, ex p Snelson* [1977] 1 WLR 911.

[32]   *R v Bennet and Bond, ex p Bennet* (1908) 72 JP 362.

[33]   *Dabhade* [1993] QB 329.

(7) the withdrawal of a charge in the magistrates' court before the defendant has pleaded to it;[34]

(8) the entering of a nolle prosequi;[35]

(9) an order that a count (or an indictment) lie on the file, not to be proceeded with without the consent of the court or the Court of Appeal;

(10) the taking of an offence into consideration when sentencing for another offence.[36]

3.35 For the purpose of the Convention, it seems acceptable to treat these various situations as falling short of a "final" acquittal or conviction. Although there is no authority directly in point, guidance can be obtained from decisions on other articles.[37] In the context of Article 5,[38] it has been held that "conviction ... has to be understood as signifying both a 'finding of guilt', after 'it has been established in accordance with the law that there has been an offence' and the imposition of a penalty or other measure".[39]

3.36 The jurisprudence on Article 6 is also of relevance, in that the article relates to the "*determination* of ... any criminal charge". The Court and the Commission have found that the right in Article 6(1) to the determination of a criminal charge does not prevent the prosecution from withdrawing an indictment or abandoning a criminal charge without a ruling, even where the effect of doing so is to deprive the defendant of a formal acquittal.[40] The Commission has also accepted a procedure under which a prosecution was adjourned sine die, subject to a prosecution undertaking not to proceed on the charges.[41]

---

[34] *R v Grays JJ, ex p Low* [1990] QB 54.

[35] *Ridpath* (1713) 10 Mod 152.

[36] *Nicholson* [1947] 2 All ER 535.

[37] The Strasbourg institutions have developed "autonomous" meanings for key terms. While the Court will use the relevant national classification as a starting point, it will look behind appearances and examine the reality of the procedure in question: see *Engels v The Netherlands (No 1)* A 22 (1976) paras 80 to 81 for an explanation of the Court's approach, in this case to the word "criminal" in Article 6. Thus, in *Gradinger* A 328-C (1995), the Court, having found that the "administrative offence" fell within the autonomous meaning of "criminal charge" for the purpose of Article 6, assumed (without further discussion) that it involved "criminal proceedings" for the purpose of Article 4.

[38] The right to liberty and security of the person.

[39] *Van Droogenbroeck v Belgium* A 50 (1982) para 35, citing *Guzzardi v Italy* A 39 (1980) para 100. The imposition of a penalty (and one involving the deprivation of liberty) is clearly of greater importance in the context of Article 5. It is nevertheless a component of the autonomous meaning of "conviction", and is likely to be so in Article 4 as well as Article 5.

[40] *X,Y and Z v Austria* (1980) 19 DR 213; *Deweer v Belgium* A 35 (1980).

[41] *X v UK* (1979) 17 DR 122. Although the charges remained on the file, the undertaking amounted in effect to the dropping of the charges: "as from [the prosecution's undertaking], there are in fact no longer any charges against the applicant which require a determination" (para 68).

Acquittal or conviction invalid

3.37 Although Article 4(2) makes specific provision for reopening in the case of a "fundamental defect", a retrial following the quashing of a summary acquittal or conviction by certiorari for excess of jurisdiction must, in our view, be outside the scope of Article 4 altogether. This is because certiorari will only be granted where the magistrates have acted in excess of their jurisdiction, not merely because they exercised it wrongly.

Retrial after appeal against conviction

3.38 Where the Court of Appeal allows an appeal against conviction on indictment, the quashing of the conviction amounts to an acquittal, but the court may order a retrial. We believe that a retrial in these circumstances does not infringe Article 4(1) because the quashing of a conviction does not amount to a *final* acquittal if it is accompanied by an order for a retrial. The appeal and the order for retrial are part of the "ordinary remedies" following the decision; until they are complete, the matter is not yet res judicata.[42]

Tainted acquittals

3.39 As already explained, this procedure permits an acquittal to be reopened on the ground that someone has been convicted of intimidating or interfering with a juror or witness in the proceedings which resulted in the acquittal.[43] In our view this is permissible under Article 4(2), because the fact that jurors or witnesses have been intimidated or interfered with must amount to a "fundamental defect" in the proceedings.

3.40 A more difficult question is whether the existing procedure for invoking this exception is in every respect compatible with the other provisions of the ECHR. In particular it is doubtful whether the procedure complies with Article 6. We consider this question in Part VI below.

Double jeopardy permitted as an exception to the Connelly *principle*

3.41 As we have seen, where a new charge is based on the same facts as a previous charge, but for a different offence, the proceedings may be justified, as an exception to the *Connelly* principle, if there are "special circumstances".[44] This presents no problem under the interpretation of Article 4(1) in *Oliveira v Switzerland*,[45] under which Article 4(1) applies only where the defendant is charged with the same offence as before. There is no need to rely on Article 4(2) to justify the "special circumstances" exception, since the case is outside Article 4 altogether.

3.42 Under the interpretation in *Gradinger v Austria*,[46] however, Article 4(1) also applies where the charge is of a different offence based on the same facts. In that

---

[42] See Explanatory Report, para 3.7 above.

[43] Criminal Procedure and Investigations Act 1996, ss 54–55. See paras 2.15 – 2.18 above.

[44] See para 2.21 above.

[45] 1998-V p 1990. See para 3.22 above.

[46] A 328-C (1995). See para 3.20 above.

26

case, the exception for "special circumstances" is acceptable only if it is limited to the circumstances in which double jeopardy is permitted by Article 4(2). To the extent that the term "special circumstances" is wider than this, there is a possibility that English law may be more permissive of double jeopardy than the ECHR allows.

Double jeopardy permitted by the ECHR but not by English law

3.43 In the light of the above, there appear to be three situations in which double jeopardy is, at least arguably, permissible under the ECHR but not (or only to a limited extent) under English law – namely:

(1) where the offence charged is not the same as the one of which the defendant has previously been acquitted or convicted;

(2) where there is evidence of new or newly discovered facts; and

(3) where there was a fundamental defect in the previous proceedings.

Of these cases, the first arguably falls outside Article 4 altogether. In the second and third cases, fresh proceedings are prohibited by Article 4(1), but the reopening of the original proceedings is permitted under Article 4(2).

Different offence

3.44 On the narrower interpretation in *Oliveira v Switzerland*,[47] the ECHR does not protect a defendant from being prosecuted again after being acquitted of a different offence on the same facts. English law does give a defendant substantial protection in this situation, because the proceedings should be stayed unless they are justified by special circumstances. However, we provisionally believe that it would be prudent to proceed on the assumption that *Gradinger v Austria*[48] represents the better view; and that the "special circumstances" exception should accordingly be treated as contrary to Article 4, in so far as it goes beyond the cases in which double jeopardy is permitted by Article 4(2). This does not necessarily imply a need for legislative change. Once the Human Rights Act is in force, the courts will be bound to give effect to the Convention rights. They may be expected, therefore, to ensure that "special circumstances" are limited to those exceptions permitted by Article 4.

Evidence of new or newly discovered facts

3.45 In English law the discovery of new evidence is not a ground for permitting a defendant to be tried again for an offence of which he or she has previously been acquitted or convicted. The autrefois rule is subject to no such exception. Article 4(2), on the other hand, would permit the reopening of an acquittal in these circumstances. This is the most striking difference between the two rules.

3.46 If the prosecution seeks to charge the defendant with a *different* offence arising out of the same facts, the discovery of the new evidence might be treated as a "special circumstance" justifying that course, by way of exception to the *Connelly* principle;

---

[47] 1998-V p 1990. See paras 3.22 – 3.24 above.

[48] A 328-C (1995). See para 3.20 above.

but this would be a matter for the court to decide. Article 4(2) would allow the acquittal to be reopened without any requirement that the circumstances be "special". The practical difference is probably not great.

Fundamental defect in the previous proceedings

3.47 Leaving aside those defects which can be corrected on appeal, such as errors of law by magistrates, the only case in which English law allows the prosecution to reopen a case on the ground of a "fundamental defect" in the proceedings is that of a tainted acquittal. Article 4(2) allows this in the case of *any* such defect. But intimidation of, and interference with, jurors and witnesses would seem to be the main examples of a defect in the proceedings which might justify another prosecution. Moreover, if the defect is so fundamental as to nullify the acquittal altogether, such as a lack of jurisdiction, the autrefois rule will not apply. But there may be defects which, while not so serious as to nullify the acquittal, would count as a fundamental defect within the meaning of Article 4(2). One possibility would be intimidation of, and interference with, the *judge* in the first trial. Another would be the case where intimidation or interference can be proved, but has not been the subject of a conviction. We discuss in Part VI ways in which the relevant provisions of the 1996 Act might be extended.

3.48 If the prosecution sought to charge the defendant with a different offence arising out of the same facts, on the ground of a fundamental defect in the previous proceedings, English law would allow this only if the defect in the previous proceedings were, in the opinion of the court, a "special circumstance" justifying that course. Article 4(2) would allow the acquittal to be reopened in any event. Again there may be little or no difference in practice. It seems unlikely that something might count as a fundamental defect but not as a special circumstance.

Conclusion

3.49 This analysis suggests that English law is generally compliant with the ECHR. Indeed, in some respects it is less permissive of double jeopardy than the ECHR, in that the autrefois rule is not subject to an exception for new evidence, or for fundamental defects in the previous proceedings other than those catered for by the provisions on tainted acquittals; and possibly also in that new evidence and fundamental defect might not be regarded as "special circumstances" for the purposes of the *Connelly* principle (though in this case the difference may be more theoretical than real).

3.50 There is a possibility of non-compliance in one respect, if the wider interpretation of Article 4(1) advanced in *Gradinger v Austria*[49] is correct. That arises if the prosecution seeks to bring proceedings for a different offence based on the same facts, and the court allows this on the basis of "special circumstances" which do not amount to new evidence or fundamental defect. On the *Gradinger* interpretation, Article 4(1) would make it unlawful for a court to do this.

---

[49] A 328-C (1995). See para 3.20 above.

PART IV
THE SCOPE OF THE RULE AGAINST DOUBLE JEOPARDY

4.1 The ECHR requires us to have a rule against double jeopardy. The question we tackle in this part is: what should be the scope of that rule?[1] It is not possible simply to implement the ECHR rule, because the scope of that rule is not clear. The two decided cases on this point appear to us (as they did to Judge Repik in his dissenting judgment in *Oliveira*)[2] to contradict one another.

4.2 The choice, however, is clear. There are two options.

(1) A narrow rule, that a person may not be tried for an offence if he or she has previously been acquitted or convicted of *the same offence* in relation to the same or substantially the same facts.[3] The scope of such a rule would be the same as that of the existing autrefois rule.[4] It would also correspond to the interpretation of Article 4(1) apparently adopted in *Oliveira*.

(2) An extended rule, that a person may not be tried for an offence if he or she has previously been acquitted or convicted of *any* offence based on the same or substantially the same facts. Unlike the narrow rule, this would extend to a prosecution for an offence which

(a) includes a lesser offence of which the defendant has previously been acquitted or convicted;[5] or

(b) though based on the same or substantially the same facts as an offence of which the defendant has previously been acquitted or convicted, neither includes nor is included in that offence.[6]

The effect would be to require all offences relating to the same or substantially the same facts to be tried together. In English law, this rule

---

[1] The question of what *exceptions* the rule should have is considered in Parts V and VI below.

[2] 1998-V p 1990. See paras 3.19 – 3.27 above.

[3] This would cover a defendant previously convicted of an offence in which the offence now charged is included (because the greater offence includes the lesser), and a defendant previously *acquitted* of such an offence (because the defendant could have been convicted of the lesser offence on an indictment charging the greater, and is therefore taken to have been acquitted of the lesser).

[4] *Beedie* [1998] QB 356, adopting the reasoning of Lord Devlin in *Connelly* [1964] AC 1254: see paras 2.3 – 2.5 above.

[5] Thus it would absorb the rule in *Elrington* (1861) 1 B & S; 121 ER 170, which prohibits successive prosecutions for the same conduct on an ascending scale of seriousness: see para 2.26 above.

[6] As in *Beedie* [1998] QB 356, where a conviction of a minor, regulatory offence barred a prosecution for a much more serious offence.

would replace both the autrefois rule *and* the *Connelly*[7] principle. It would also correspond to the interpretation of Article 4(1) adopted in *Gradinger*.[8]

4.3 For the purpose of determining which rule to adopt, in this part we examine the justifications commonly advanced for having a double jeopardy rule at all, and consider whether they justify the extended rule or only the narrow rule. In the light of our terms of reference, our primary focus is on the rule as it relates to acquittals; but we also address arguments relating to convictions, where they seem to be different.

THE JUSTIFICATIONS FOR THE DOUBLE JEOPARDY RULE

4.4 We now consider the justifications generally advanced for a rule against double jeopardy, and whether they would justify the extended form of that rule.

The risk of wrongful conviction

4.5 Black J, whom we quoted at the start of this paper,[9] saw repeated trials as increasing the likelihood of wrongful conviction. For Friedland, this point "is at the core of the problem", as "[i]n many cases an innocent person will not have the stamina or resources effectively to fight a second charge".[10] In England and Wales, lack of *financial* resources is not usually a serious problem for defendants in criminal cases because of the availability of legal aid. But the risk of wrongful conviction must be increased to some extent by any retrial. If it is accepted that juries do on occasion return perverse verdicts of guilty,[11] the chance that a particular defendant will be perversely convicted must increase if he or she is tried more than once. Moreover, because there has already been one trial at which the defence has shown its hand, the prosecution may enjoy a tactical advantage at a second trial; and this will increase the likelihood of a conviction, whether the defendant is guilty or innocent.[12] These arguments may or may not be compelling. For present purposes it is sufficient to point out that, in so far as they are valid, they apply equally whether the retrial is for the same offence or for a different offence on the same facts. If they justify the narrow rule, they justify the extended rule too.

---

[7] [1964] AC 1254: see paras 2.21 – 2.22 above.

[8] A 328-C (1995). See para 3.20 above.

[9] Para 1.2 above.

[10] *Double Jeopardy* (1969) p 4.

[11] That is, a guilty verdict where there was nothing in the trial process, save the result, that could raise a ground of appeal – a case which would fall only into the category formerly described as "lurking doubt" cases, such as *Cooper* [1969] 1 QB 267.

[12] The same point could be made in relation to a retrial where the jury has failed to agree.

The distress of the trial process

4.6 Black J's statement[13] refers to the exposure of the defendant to "embarrassment, expense and ordeal and compelling him to live in a continuing state of anxiety and insecurity". Similarly, Glanville Williams has written:

> It is hard on the defendant if, after he has at great cost in money and anxiety secured a favourable verdict from a jury on a particular issue, he must fight the battle over again when he is charged with a technically different offence arising out of the same facts.[14]

The cost in money may not be of great significance in this country because of the availability of legal aid, but the cost in anxiety may well be. In 1907 the Lord Chancellor, Lord Loreburn, said that "it approaches the confines of torture to put a man on trial twice for the same offence".[15]

4.7 It cannot be doubted that facing trial, at least for a serious offence, must be extremely distressing. This distress is not confined to the defendant. His or her family also suffers, as do witnesses on both sides, including the alleged victim. We believe that this is a powerful consideration, and that it justifies not only the narrow rule against double jeopardy but also the extended rule. The argument is that a person should not be put in jeopardy for a second time because of the distress and trauma of the trial process; and that distress is likely to be much the same whether the second trial is for the same offence or for a different offence arising out of the same facts.[16]

The need for finality

4.8 It is sometimes said that the public interest requires finality in litigation, including criminal litigation,[17] and that this justifies the double jeopardy rule. It is certainly an important principle in *civil* proceedings, where the ownership of property or contractual relations must be settled to protect the interests of third parties. In the

---

[13] Para 1.2 above.

[14] *Textbook of Criminal Law* (2nd ed 1983) p 164. This particular statement relates only to cases falling within the *Connelly* principle, but clearly the principle also applies to true autrefois cases.

[15] *Hansard* 5 August 1907, vol 179, col 1473.

[16] It is true that, in a case caught only by the extended rule, the second charge may be much more serious than the first. In *Beedie* [1998] QB 356, for example, the defendant first pleaded guilty to summary offences under the Health and Safety at Work Act 1974, and was subsequently charged with manslaughter on the basis of the same incident. On the assumption that the summary charges were less distressing for him than the manslaughter charge, it follows that the total distress caused by both trials was less than if they had both been for manslaughter. From this point of view, the extended rule, which would protect the defendant in such a case, is arguably less necessary than the narrow rule, which would protect him against being tried twice for manslaughter. But the narrow rule would also protect him from being tried twice for the summary offences, which would presumably have been *less* distressing than the course actually taken. Arguably, therefore, the case for protecting him should be all the stronger where the second charge is for a more serious offence than the first.

[17] It was, for instance, the primary argument used by those who opposed the introduction of a general right of appeal against conviction on indictment in the Criminal Appeal Act 1907.

criminal context the advantages of finality may be less tangible; but here too we believe that there is virtue in putting a line under emotive and contentious events, so that life can move on. However, this consideration may well be outweighed by others, such as the need to avoid miscarriages of justice. Where it transpires that a person has been wrongly *convicted*, there is no question of preserving that unjust outcome in the interests of finality. And the need for finality is not generally thought to justify a time limit for the prosecution of serious offences.

4.9 Finality may also be important in a rather different sense, namely that its absence may be unfair to the defendant. The autrefois rule means that, once a defendant has been acquitted (or convicted and sentenced), he or she knows that that is the end of the matter. In a serious case, the prospect of going through the trial process at some future date is likely to cause great anxiety, both for the defendant and for others involved. At least some acquitted defendants will be prey to a constant and persisting sense of doubt. As an American author puts it, in the context of sentence, there is a

> need for "repose", a desire to know the exact extent of one's liability, an interest in knowing "once and for all" how many years one will have to spend in prison.[18]

Lack of such "repose" can be debilitating and disturbing.

4.10 This argument is clearly related to the argument based on the distress caused by the trial process itself, and again we believe that it justifies the extended rule as well as the narrow rule. Where it is possible to charge two or more offences arising out of a single event, but not all are in fact charged, the extended rule would protect the acquitted defendant from continuing uncertainty in relation to the offence or offences not originally charged.

The need to encourage efficient investigation

4.11 If the prosecution could re-prosecute an acquitted defendant, there is a danger that the initial investigation might not be as diligent as it would otherwise be. At present, the fact that there is but one chance to convict a defendant operates as a powerful incentive to efficient and exhaustive investigation. This argument applies with equal force to the extended rule. In general the police should be expected to investigate *all* aspects of an incident which may have involved the commission of crime. Similarly, the prosecution should properly assess what offences to charge, and should then seek to have them tried together wherever possible.[19]

CONCLUSIONS

4.12 In our view, therefore, the considerations that justify the narrow rule against double jeopardy are equally applicable to the extended rule. What are the consequences of this conclusion?

---

[18] P Westen, "The Three Faces of Double Jeopardy: Reflections On Government Appeals of Criminal Sentence" 78 Michigan Law Review 1001 (1980).

[19] This argument does not apply to private prosecutions.

The current law

4.13 The current law is in effect a halfway house between the narrow rule and the extended rule. There is already a narrow rule, namely the autrefois rule. And there is already a rule, albeit a more flexible one, applying to those cases that would be caught by the extended rule but not the narrow rule – namely the *Connelly* principle. If, as we suggest, the justifications for the two rules are effectively the same, it is difficult to see why there should be two rules, with different effects, rather than one. If the considerations applicable to cases falling within the autrefois rule are equally applicable to cases falling within the *Connelly* principle, in our view the law should treat both kinds of case in the same way.

A statutory rule

4.14 The replacement of two rules with one would obviously require legislation. It does not follow that the legislation should have to incorporate a complete statement of the rule, together with any exceptions to which the rule might be subject. For example, the legislation might extend the autrefois rule to cases which at present fall within the *Connelly* principle, while leaving the rule itself as part of the common law. We do not favour this approach. It is the objective of this Commission to secure codification of the criminal law, including matters of procedure.[20] In general we believe that codification makes the law clearer, simpler and more accessible. It follows that in our view it would be preferable to enact the rule against double jeopardy in statutory form, rather than leaving it as part of the common law.

4.15 This is particularly so if the rule is to be subject to exceptions, which must themselves be in statutory form. The two existing rules are already subject to exceptions. The tainted acquittal provisions provide an exception to the autrefois rule, and the *Connelly* principle is subject to "special circumstances". Later in this paper, we propose adding a further exception to the new rule.[21] The scope and content of the existing rules and their exceptions, and related rules,[22] and the relationship between them, is not always clear. We believe that in terms of clarity and accessibility they would benefit from codification – particularly (but not only) if the exceptions were extended and modified in the ways we later propose.

4.16 **We provisionally propose that**

    (1) **the rule against double jeopardy should be retained;**

    (2) **the rule should be extended so as to prohibit the prosecution of a person not only**

        (a) **for any offence of which he or she has previously been acquitted or convicted, but also**

        (b) **for any offence founded on the same or substantially the same facts as such an offence; and**

    (3) **the rule as thus extended, and any exceptions to it, should be stated in statutory form.**

---

[20] A definition of the autrefois rule was included as clause 11 of our draft criminal code: A Criminal Code for England and Wales (1989) Law Com No 177. The contents of the rule have been overtaken by the development of the case law since that time.

[21] See Part V below.

[22] Eg that in *Sambasivam* [1950] AC 458; see Part VIII below.

PART V
NEW EVIDENCE

5.1 So far in this paper we have argued that double jeopardy should, in general, continue to be prohibited by English law, particularly since this is necessitated by the incorporation of the ECHR; that the present autrefois rule should be put into statutory form; and that it should be extended in its scope. We now consider whether the rule, as extended, should be an *absolute* bar to the reopening of a prosecution after an acquittal has become res judicata, or whether it should be subject to any exceptions. Article 4(2) permits two kinds of exception: where there are "new or newly discovered facts", and where there was a "fundamental defect" in the first trial. In this part we consider whether English law should recognise an exception in the former case, before turning in Part VI to the latter.

5.2 We begin by pointing out that double jeopardy may already be permissible where, on the basis of new evidence, it is proposed to prosecute a person who has previously been acquitted or convicted of a different offence on the same facts. The question, therefore, is whether this possibility should be extended to the case where the defendant has previously been acquitted of the *same* offence. We then consider whether it is possible to imagine any case in which new evidence would justify a second trial for the same offence. For this purpose we hypothesise the strongest possible case for allowing a retrial; and we provisionally conclude that in such a case a retrial would be justified. We then examine each of the features that make our hypothetical case a particularly strong one, and discuss whether a retrial would still be justified if that feature were absent. In the light of this discussion we provisionally propose that there should be an exception for new evidence, but that it should be subject to various safeguards which would ensure that it could be invoked only in exceptional circumstances.

5.3 Having accepted the principle, we turn to the procedure. We propose that the court empowered to quash an acquittal on grounds of new evidence should be the High Court; that the hearing should be in open court, with both parties represented and witnesses heard and cross-examined; and that there should be a right of appeal against the quashing of an acquittal to the Court of Appeal, Criminal Division. Finally we consider how our proposals should apply in a case where evidence of a serious offence is discovered after the defendant has been *convicted* of another, less serious offence on the same or substantially the same facts.

THE ISSUE

5.4 In his reference, the Home Secretary particularly asked us to take account of recommendation 38 of the Macpherson Report, which specifically suggests the possibility of the Court of Appeal being given power to permit prosecution after acquittal where there is "fresh and viable" evidence. But it should be noted that in some cases such a power already exists. Where a person is acquitted or convicted and is later charged with a *different offence* on the same or substantially the same facts, the second prosecution can be allowed to proceed if there are special circumstances which satisfactorily explain why the second charge was not brought

34

at the same time as the first.[1] One such explanation, clearly, is the fact that, when the first charge was brought, the prosecution did not have enough evidence to bring the second. It follows that, where evidence of an offence is discovered after the acquittal or conviction of the apparent offender on another charge arising out of the same or substantially the same facts, the court can allow a prosecution for the second offence to proceed; and there is recent authority to this effect.[2] Thus, while the finding of new evidence does not at present constitute an exception to the narrow autrefois rule, the wider *Connelly* principle is already subject to such an exception (though its limits are not clearly defined). The question is whether that exception should be retained; and, if so, whether it should be *extended* to cases which now fall within the narrow autrefois rule, and what should be its limits.

CAN NEW EVIDENCE *EVER* JUSTIFY A RETRIAL FOR THE SAME OFFENCE?

5.5   Article 4(1) of the ECHR *requires* signatory states to have a rule against double jeopardy. Article 4(2) *permits* them to have certain exceptions to that rule. Our interpretation is that each state is free to decide whether its rule against double jeopardy should be subject to these exceptions. It is true that victims are entitled to have their Convention rights protected by the enactment of appropriate laws[3] and the enforcement of the criminal law.[4] But we do not believe that the state has any duty to reopen a prosecution, or to institute a procedure to allow for such reopening. This would mean that any divergence from a single correct path would infringe the rights of *either* the victim *or* the defendant. Even the state's obligation to protect an individual's right to life "must be interpreted in a way which does not impose an impossible or disproportionate burden on the authorities".[5]

5.6   We therefore conclude that it would be permissible under the ECHR to extend the new evidence exception to cases which now fall within the narrow autrefois rule, but there is no compulsion to do so. We must therefore consider whether it would be in the interests of justice to do so. The approach we adopt is to ask first whether it is possible to imagine *any* circumstances in which it might be justifiable to retry a person for an offence of which he or she has previously been acquitted, on the ground that new evidence has since become available. For this purpose we assume the existence of circumstances in which the case for reopening is as strong as it could realistically be. If our conclusion were that even in these circumstances it should be impossible to reopen the acquittal, obviously we would not need to consider circumstances in which the case for reopening is weaker.

[1]   *Connelly v DPP* [1964] AC 1254, *per* Lord Devlin, whose reasoning was adopted in *Beedie* [1998] QB 356: see para 2.21 above.

[2]   *Attorney General for Gibraltar v Leoni*, Criminal Appeal No 4 of 1998, judgment given 19 March 1999; unreported. See para 2.24 above.

[3]   *A v UK* 1998-VI p 2692.

[4]   See, eg, *Aydin v Turkey* 1997-VI p 1866, paras 99–109 (the conclusion being put in terms of Article 13, which is not a "Convention right" within the terms of the Human Rights Act 1998); *McCann v UK* A 324 (1995), paras 146, 161; *Osman v UK* 28 October 1998, para 115; *Oður v Turkey* 20 May 1999, para 93; *Assenov v Bulgaria* [1999] EHRLR 225.

[5]   *Osman v UK* 28 October 1998, para 116.

The strongest case

5.7   The features of the strongest possible case for reopening an acquittal on grounds of new evidence, we suggest, are as follows:

    (1)   The offence with which it is sought to charge the defendant is a serious one.[6]

    (2)   The new evidence is very strong.

    (3)   It was not through any want of diligence that the new evidence was not available at the time of the first trial.

    (4)   Leaving aside those considerations that render double jeopardy *generally* undesirable, on the facts of the individual case there is no particular reason why it might be contrary to the interests of justice to subject the defendant to a retrial.

5.8   The sort of case we have in mind is illustrated by the following examples.

    (a)   In a rape case, the complainant identifies the defendant, whom she did not know, and there is circumstantial evidence implicating him. The defendant claims that he has never met the complainant, and puts up an alibi. Some body fluid is found which unquestionably came from the rapist, but the quantity is too small to permit DNA analysis. The defendant is acquitted. Three months later, a new DNA test becomes available which makes it possible to analyse much smaller quantities of biological material than had formerly been the case.[7] The technique is used to identify the rapist's body fluid as coming from the defendant.

    (b)   Two defendants are acquitted of conspiracy to murder. They are alleged to have hired X to kill another. The prosecution case, while to a degree compelling, is purely circumstantial. Shortly after the trial, as a consequence of a genuine religious conversion, X comes forward and volunteers to give evidence for the prosecution. The veracity of her evidence is supported by the revelation of certain details that would only be known to the murderer.

The question is whether it is right that, even in a case as strong as these, it should be impossible to reopen the acquittal.

---

[6]   The case for reopening would arguably be even stronger if the charge of which the defendant was acquitted (or, as in *Beedie* [1998] QB 356, convicted), though arising out of the same or substantially the same facts as the charge it is now sought to bring, was for a different and much less serious offence. In these circumstances the argument that the defendant should not be twice subjected to the distress of a trial seems less cogent. But it seems that there is *already* a new evidence exception in this kind of case: see para 5.2 above. The case we now postulate is the strongest one *currently caught by the autrefois rule*, which is subject to no such exception. We must therefore assume that the charge it is now sought to bring is for the same offence as the one of which the defendant was previously acquitted.

[7]   See for instance the technique discussed in *Police Review* 16 April 1999.

The justifications for the rule

5.9   To answer that question, we turn again to the justifications that have been advanced for the double jeopardy rule, and which we examined in Part IV above. Do these arguments justify an *absolute* bar on the re-opening of a prosecution, even in circumstances such as those of the hypothetical cases described in the previous paragraph?

The risk of wrongful conviction

5.10   One justification for the rule against double jeopardy is the fact that any retrial of an acquitted defendant must to some extent increase the risk of that defendant being wrongly convicted.[8] But this is equally true of any trial. In general the law seeks to minimise the risk of convicting the innocent without making it unacceptably hard to convict the guilty. The question is whether that objective justifies a rule which prevents an acquittal from ever being reopened, even in circumstances such as those of our strongest case. One of the features of that case is that the new evidence is very strong. It follows that the risk of *wrongful* conviction at a retrial would be very small – considerably smaller than in the ordinary case, where the prosecution's evidence need only constitute a case to answer.

The distress of the trial process

5.11   Another justification for the rule against double jeopardy is the distress likely to be occasioned by a second trial.[9] But any trial is likely to cause distress to the defendant. In general the law takes the view that, where there is a case to answer,[10] that distress may be outweighed by the public interest in the conviction of the guilty. The question here is whether a case can ever be strong enough to justify the distress of a *second* trial. The answer implicit in the autrefois rule is that it cannot. We believe that this exaggerates the difference between the distress caused by one trial and the distress caused by two. This is an important difference, in our view, and one which justifies a much stricter requirement as to the strength of the prosecution's case; but it is a difference only of degree. We believe that a case *can* be strong enough to justify putting a defendant through the anxiety and distress of a second trial; and we believe that our hypothetical examples, being as strong as can realistically be imagined, *would* be strong enough to justify this. The anxiety and distress occasioned by trial justifies a *general* rule against retrials, but not, in our view, an *absolute* one.

5.12   In fact, the present law does sometimes allow retrials. There is a prosecution right of appeal on a point of law to the Divisional Court from acquittal in the magistrates' court, one result of which may be a new trial.[11] The Court of Appeal

---

[8]   See para 4.5 above.

[9]   See paras 4.6 above.

[10]   In the case of summary trial there is no preliminary testing of the strength of the prosecution case at all, though it can be submitted at the close of the prosecution's evidence that there is no case to answer.

[11]   See para 2.12 above.

can order a retrial when it allows an appeal against conviction. There can be a second (or even a third)[12] trial on indictment if the jury fail to agree. It is difficult to see why the distress caused by a retrial should be any less in these cases than where a retrial follows an acquittal.

5.13 It is true that, in a particular case, the distress likely to be caused by a retrial might be out of all proportion to the seriousness of the alleged crime, or the public interest in the conviction of offenders. This may be an argument for confining the exception to serious offences, or preserving a discretion not to allow a second trial if this does not appear to be in the interests of justice. These are issues we consider below.[13]

The need for finality

5.14 As we noted in Part IV, one virtue of a rule against double jeopardy is that, once acquitted or convicted, a defendant will not be prey to continuing anxiety and distress occasioned by the *fear* that, at some time in the future, he or she will again be prosecuted for the same offence.[14] In assessing the force of this argument in relation to our hypothetical strongest case, it is important to recall that the reopening of a prosecution would by its nature be a very occasional occurrence. To be compliant with Article 4, the reopening must be an extraordinary rather than an ordinary procedure.[15] Arguably, the only defendants who would be likely to fear retrial after being once acquitted are those who are in fact guilty, because only they would be likely to suspect the existence of further evidence which might one day be found. And it is not obviously undesirable that such defendants should be subjected to the anxiety of knowing that their crimes may eventually be punished.

5.15 We accept this argument to a degree. But we must recognise that we are not dealing only with rational responses. Once there is a widely recognised exception to the double jeopardy rule, there is a danger that anyone who does not fully understand the safeguards might entertain a lingering *and ill-founded* fear of being prosecuted again. One way of meeting this difficulty would be to make the new exception subject to a time limit, and we consider this possibility below.[16] Where there is a balance to be struck between the interest of the defendant in finality and the public interest in the conviction of the guilty, it must be relevant whether a new exception would make finality permanently unattainable, or merely delay it for a time.

---

[12] Though in practice the prosecution generally does not seek a third trial where two juries have failed to agree.

[13] See paras 5.19 – 5.29, 5.49 – 5.51 and Part VII below.

[14] See paras 4.9 – 4.10 above.

[15] See para 3.28 above.

[16] See paras 5.52 – 5.57 below.

The need to encourage efficient investigation

5.16 We accepted in Part IV that the encouragement of efficient investigation is a sound argument for a double jeopardy rule, even if less important than those above.[17] It is a component of our hypothetical strongest case that it was not for want of diligence that the new evidence was not available at the time of the first trial. In our view this argument therefore does not militate against allowing a retrial in such circumstances as these.

Conclusion

5.17 In our provisional view, the justifications for a rule against double jeopardy do not require that it should be impossible to reopen the acquittal in circumstances such as those of our hypothetical strongest case. It does not seem to us unfair or unjust that, in the examples in paragraph 5.8 above, the rapist or the conspirators should face retrial. We conclude that there should not be an *absolute* bar to the reopening of an acquittal on grounds of new evidence; and that this is so irrespective of whether, in the light of the new evidence, the prosecution now seeks a conviction for a different offence on the same facts (which it may already be permitted to do, by way of exception to the *Connelly* principle) or for the same offence (which, at present, it may not). **We provisionally propose that the rule against double jeopardy should be subject to an exception for certain cases where new evidence is discovered after an acquittal.** We now go on to consider what the terms of such an exception should be.

THE TERMS ON WHICH REOPENING MIGHT BE PERMITTED

5.18 If, in our hypothetical strongest case, the public interest in the prosecution of alleged crime is strong enough to justify an exception to the double jeopardy rule, would this also be true in a case where that public interest is less strong? To answer this question, we now examine the elements of our strongest case and consider whether, even in the absence of each such element, the reopening of an acquittal might still be justified.

The seriousness of the offence

5.19 In our hypothetical strongest case, the offence of which the defendant has previously been acquitted, and for which it is now sought to bring further proceedings, is a serious offence. We must now consider whether the reopening of an acquittal should be permitted *only* in the case of such an offence.

5.20 Clearly the public interest in the prosecution of an alleged offender is at its greatest when the alleged offence is a very serious one. In the case of a comparatively minor offence, the public interest in reopening an acquittal is likely to be less strong. It is more important to correct an undeserved acquittal of murder than one of petty theft.

5.21 On the other hand, we have argued that the main factor which justifies the rule against double jeopardy, and which militates against the creation of an exception

---

[17] Para 4.11 above.

39

for new evidence, is the distress likely to result from being subjected to a retrial, or to the possibility of one. While there may be circumstances in which a retrial for a comparatively minor offence would be particularly distressing for a defendant,[18] in general it seems likely that the distress factor will also be at its greatest where the offence charged is very serious, and where a conviction would therefore be likely to result in a long term of imprisonment.

5.22 Thus, where the offence is a serious one, both the public interest in favour of a retrial *and* the defendant's legitimate interest in finality are greater than where the offence is comparatively minor. We have already concluded that, in a very serious case, the public interest in prosecution might outweigh the defendant's interest in finality. The question here is whether, in a less serious case, the *diminution* in the former is likely to be outweighed by the diminution in the latter; and, if so, whether the difference in weight is likely to be so great that the possibility of a retrial ought to be ruled out altogether.

5.23 Our provisional answer to both questions is yes. The standard of proof in a criminal case is, rightly, a very high one. The general public, we believe, is well aware that the evidence against a defendant will sometimes fail to satisfy that standard although the defendant is in fact guilty; and, in the ordinary run of offences against property and minor assaults, the public is generally content to accept this as the price to be paid for the presumption of innocence. It is only in the case of comparatively serious offences, we believe, that the public might be outraged if, despite the emergence of cogent new evidence of an offence, a prosecution could not be brought because the alleged offender had already been acquitted of that offence.

5.24 It is arguable that, although the public interest in a retrial is *unlikely* to outweigh the defendant's legitimate interests in a comparatively trivial case, that possibility should not be ruled out altogether. On this view, the seriousness of the alleged offence would be merely one factor for the court to take into account in deciding whether it is in the interests of justice to quash the acquittal. Our provisional answer to this argument is that it gives insufficient weight to the need for finality. An acquittal is either final or it is not; and, if it is not, even a remote possibility of its being reopened may acquire disproportionate significance in the defendant's mind. We do not believe that it would be right to subject every person acquitted of (for example) careless driving to the uncertainty of knowing that the acquittal might in theory be reopened, however unlikely that possibility might be. Our provisional conclusion, therefore, is that the possibility of reopening an acquittal should be available *only* where the offence alleged is of a certain minimum seriousness.

5.25 This conclusion raises the question of how the boundary should be drawn between those alleged offences that are sufficiently serious to justify the possibility of reopening, and those that are not. The simplest option would be to use one of the ways in which the law classifies different offences. For example, the exception

---

[18] For example, where a conviction for a road traffic offence might result in the loss of the defendant's driving licence, and therefore his or her livelihood.

might be restricted to cases where the alleged offence is triable only on indictment; or cases where it is punishable with imprisonment; or cases where it is punishable with a term of imprisonment for a stated period (say two years, or five).

5.26 Our provisional view is that this approach would be insufficiently flexible to ensure that the exception was available *only* in serious cases. Some offences are triable only on indictment, and carry a very severe maximum sentence, although a particular example of them might attract comparatively little blame.[19] We do not think it would be fair to the defendant for the new evidence exception to be even theoretically available in such a case. The objective is to ensure that the exception is available only where the alleged offence is, *on the alleged facts*, a serious one. It seems to us that the way to achieve this objective is for the availability of the exception to depend not on the sentence which a court could in theory impose, but on the sentence which it would in fact be likely to impose, in the event of a conviction.

5.27 **We provisionally propose that**

(1)   the exception for new evidence should be available only where, if the defendant were convicted of the offence now alleged, the sentence would be likely to be of a specified minimum severity; and

(2)   for the purpose of determining what sentence would be likely to be imposed, it should be assumed

(a)   that the plea would be one of not guilty;

(b)   that the court would find the facts to be as the prosecution now alleges them to be; and

(c)   that the sentence would not be reduced on the basis of any distress or uncertainty resulting from the retrial, or the lapse of time since the offence or the acquittal.

5.28 The next question is what the specified minimum sentence should be. This is very much a matter of judgment, and one on which we do not feel especially well qualified to pronounce. But we would suggest that a case should *not* be subject to the exception if, were a prosecution allowed, it would not even result in a sentence of imprisonment. We would also suggest that a case *should* be subject to the exception (assuming that the other conditions are satisfied) if it would probably attract five or more years' imprisonment: otherwise a "typical" rape case, with no aggravating features, would be excluded,[20] and we think this would be

---

[19]   A striking example is manslaughter, which "ranges in its gravity from the borders of murder right down to those of accidental death": *Walker* (1992) 13 Cr App R (S) 474, 476, *per* Lord Lane CJ. See our report Legislating the Criminal Code: Involuntary Manslaughter (1996) Law Com No 237.

[20]   In *Billam* (1986) 8 Cr App R (S) 48 the Court of Appeal said: "For rape committed by an adult without any aggravating or mitigating features, a figure of five years should be taken as the starting point in a contested case."

inappropriate. Within that range, we invite suggestions as to what the minimum should be. For the benefit of respondents unfamiliar with current sentencing practice, at Appendix C to this paper we give examples of the sort of conduct that would be likely to attract different sentences within the range that we have identified.

5.29 **We invite views on what, for the purpose of the proposal at paragraph 5.27 above, the specified minimum sentence should be. Our provisional preference is for a minimum of three years' imprisonment.**

The strength of the evidence

5.30 In our hypothetical strongest case, the new evidence was very strong, and our provisional view is that this should be a prerequisite for the application of the new exception. An acquitted defendant should not be subjected to a second trial unless there is clear justification for doing so; and we do not think that the discovery of new evidence could amount to such justification if its probative value is small. But we must consider what such a requirement might involve. Where new evidence has come to light, what does it mean to say that the evidence is very strong?

Two kinds of strength: reliability and relevance

5.31 It should first be noted that the strength of a given piece of evidence usually has two aspects. In the first place, the evidence can be strong in the sense of credible and reliable; that is, evidence which the trier of fact is likely to believe. Secondly, the evidence may be strong in the sense that, if accepted, it would have great probative value; that is, it would make it much more likely that the defendant is guilty (or innocent, as the case may be). The overall strength of a piece of evidence is the product of *both* these factors. It is the extent to which, taking into account the likelihood of the evidence being true, the evidence makes it more or less likely that the defendant is guilty.[21]

Assessing the strength of the new evidence

5.32 In addition to these two *kinds* of strength, there is more than one way in which the strength of new evidence might be *assessed*.

INDEPENDENT STRENGTH

5.33 One approach would be to assess the strength of the new evidence *in its own right*, independently of the evidence available at the first trial. It would in theory be possible to confine the new exception to cases where the new evidence is very strong in this sense. This would mean that the new evidence must not only be reliable but must *in itself* make it very likely that the defendant is guilty. In our view, a requirement of strength in this absolute sense would be unrealistic. Compelling evidence as to the defendant's whereabouts two hours before the offence, for example, or documentary evidence that he or she engaged in a

---

[21] There is a parallel in the factors which the Court of Appeal, Criminal Division must take into account when considering whether to admit new evidence on an appeal against conviction. One is whether the new evidence is *credible*, another is whether it *affords a ground of appeal*: Criminal Appeal Act 1968, s 23.

particular transaction, might be crucial when considered with the rest of the evidence; but on their own they would be quite meaningless. Clearly the new evidence cannot sensibly be assessed in isolation, but only in relation to the old.

ADDITIONAL STRENGTH

5.34 This consideration suggests another approach. One might assess the strength of the new evidence by asking how much *difference* it makes – that is, how much *stronger* the prosecution's case is, with the benefit of the new evidence, than it was at the first trial. The new exception might include a requirement that this difference in strength should be of some minimum degree. The exception would then be unavailable where the new evidence does not advance the prosecution's case by very much. This might be because the new evidence is unreliable, or because it would have little probative value even if it were true, or both.

5.35 It would not be necessary to include such a requirement in order to bring the new evidence exception within the terms of Article 4(2), because that requires only that the new evidence "could affect the outcome of the case"; but we think it would be desirable. On this view a retrial could be justified only if, on the basis of the evidence now available, the prosecution's case is much stronger than before. If, for example, three reputable witnesses gave credible evidence of a particular fact at the first trial, it would not seem right to hold a retrial merely because a fourth witness had come forward who could also testify to that fact.

5.36 One way of restricting the exception to new evidence which is particularly strong would be to restrict it to certain *types* of evidence which are *likely* to be particularly strong. Examples might include confession evidence or DNA evidence. There seem to us to be two problems with this approach. First, it is almost inevitable that a case will arise in which new evidence of overwhelming strength arises which does not fit within the categories identified. Secondly, not every piece of evidence within a particular type or description will necessarily be very strong. If the issue is which of two brothers raped the complainant, evidence of DNA analysis is unlikely to be of any significance. Similarly, a confession obtained by oppression is worthless. We therefore reject the possibility of isolating types of evidence of particular cogency. If it is thought that the exception should apply only where the new evidence is particularly strong, in our view this should be done by directly comparing the strength of the prosecution's case with and without the new evidence, and asking whether the difference is sufficiently great.

5.37 A possible objection to such a requirement is that, if the prosecution's case at the first trial was already very strong (albeit unsuccessful on that occasion), there might be no room for it to get much stronger. Suppose, for example, that, before the first trial, an experienced prosecutor would have estimated that nine juries out of ten would convict; and that, taking the new evidence into account, that estimate would be increased to 19 juries out of 20. The case could not be said to be *much* stronger than before. If it were thought that such a case should nevertheless be tried again, it would follow that no great increase in the strength of the case should be required, and that the *only* question should be how strong the case now is.

5.38 We accept that this is a difficulty. But the objection is valid only if the premise is accepted, namely that new evidence justifies a retrial if it makes a very strong case marginally stronger; and we do not accept that premise. The only way that new evidence can add much probative value is by helping to prove an element of the offence, or to disprove an element of a defence, on which the evidence originally adduced was deficient. If that evidence was *not* deficient (that is, the acquittal was against the weight of the evidence), and the new evidence merely makes the case marginally more overwhelming than it already was, a retrial would in substance be an appeal against the verdict on the *original* evidence, rather than a reopening of the decision on the basis of *new* evidence. It is arguable that such appeals should be permitted; but that is a different issue, and one on which we make no proposal.[22] The question here is whether such a case should fall within our proposed exception for *new* evidence, and we think it should not. **We provisionally propose that the exception for new evidence should be available only where the new evidence makes the prosecution's case substantially stronger than it was at the first trial.**[23]

OVERALL STRENGTH

5.39 It would also be possible to require (either as well as the requirement we have just proposed or instead of it) that the prosecution's case, as strengthened by the new evidence, should be of some minimum strength *overall*. If there were no such requirement, the exception might be invoked where the prosecution's case at the first trial was very weak indeed, and the new evidence makes it much stronger, but still does not turn it into a very strong case overall. In our view, cases of this kind ought not to be included within the new exception. The law generally regards the existence of a prima facie case as sufficient justification to put a person on trial, in spite of the distress that will thus be caused; but in our view this cannot be so where the proposed defendant has already been once acquitted. We think there should be a requirement that the evidence available for the retrial, *as a whole*, must be of a certain minimum strength, over and above the ordinary requirement of a prima facie case. The court considering whether to quash the acquittal would have to assess the likelihood of a conviction, by a reasonable jury properly directed, on the basis of *all* the evidence now available, and taking into account any defence that might be relied upon.

5.40 At what point should this minimum likelihood of a conviction be set? One possibility would be to require that a conviction at the ensuing retrial must be more likely than an acquittal. This would be the same test that prosecutors are currently required to apply in deciding whether there is enough evidence for a *first* prosecution.[24] It would mean that, where the prosecution's original case was very weak, the exception would be available if the new evidence strengthens the case to

---

[22] See Part XI below.

[23] This requirement would not be satisfied if the strengthening of the case by the new evidence were offset by a deterioration in any other respect – eg the unavailability of a witness whose evidence would not be admitted under ss 23 and 24 of the Criminal Justice Act 1988, or some event which undermined the credibility of a witness.

[24] Code for Crown Prosecutors (1994 ed) para 5.2. It was recently reported that there is to be consultation on whether this criterion should be relaxed: *The Times* 12 August 1999.

such an extent that a conviction at a retrial would be marginally more likely than another acquittal. Our provisional view is that it would not be justifiable to subject the defendant to the distress of a retrial in these circumstances. We think the exception should not be available unless, in the view of the court considering whether to quash the acquittal, it is at least *highly* probable (that is, *much* more probable than not) that a reasonable jury, properly directed, would convict. Arguably even this threshold is not sufficiently high, and the court should have to be *sure* that such a jury would convict.

5.41 One argument against a very high threshold is that the defendant would be prejudiced at the retrial if it were known that the High Court or the Court of Appeal had considered the evidence and, in effect, concluded that the defendant was very probably guilty. Much the same argument was deployed by those opposed to the granting of a power to the Court of Criminal Appeal to order a retrial following the allowing of an appeal against conviction.[25] But, as far as we know, these fears appear to have been groundless. This is presumably in part because the general public are unlikely to know much about decision-making in appellate courts; but also because, if the jury do learn of the previous trial, they will be directed to ignore its outcome.[26] We accept that it might be necessary to give the retrial jury strong directions, and it might also be appropriate to introduce reporting restrictions. And, most importantly, if it appeared that the risk of prejudice could not be excluded in a particular case, that would be a powerful argument on the question of whether a retrial was in the interests of justice, or in support of an application to the trial judge to stay the retrial as an abuse of process.

5.42 **We provisionally propose that the exception for new evidence should be available only where, taking into account *all* the evidence likely to be adduced, the likelihood of the defendant being convicted at a retrial is judged by the court to be of a certain minimum level. The options for this minimum level include**

    (1) that a reasonable jury, properly directed, would be more likely to convict than to acquit;

    (2) that it is highly probable that such a jury would convict; or

    (3) that the court is sure that such a jury would convict.

We provisionally reject (1), and invite views on (2) and (3).

---

[25] See for instance *Hansard* (HC) 14 April 1948, vol 449, cols 1106–1109; (HL) 1 July 1948, vol 157, cols 182–192; (HL) 8 May 1952, vol 176, cols 759–770; Report of the Departmental Committee on New Trials in Criminal Cases (1954) Cmd 9150, paras 15–16.

[26] It should also be noted that, before quashing an acquittal under the tainted acquittal procedure, the High Court is required to be satisfied that it is "likely that, but for the interference or intimidation, the acquitted person would not have been acquitted": Criminal Procedure and Investigations Act 1996, s 55(1). See paras 6.14 – 6.17 below.

Private prosecutions

5.43   It may be arguable that the need for a very strong case should be relaxed where the acquittal was the outcome of a *private* prosecution. Suppose, for example, that the CPS declines to prosecute because the evidence available does not even amount to a case to answer (let alone satisfy the stricter test of a "realistic prospect of conviction", as the Code for Crown Prosecutors requires). A private prosecution is brought, and fails as expected. New evidence is then discovered, and the CPS now believes that, if a second prosecution were permitted, there *would* be a realistic prospect of conviction; but a conviction would still be far from certain. Should the exception for new evidence be available in such a case? Can it be said that the possibility of a conviction in a public prosecution should not be ruled out by the failure of an ill-advised private prosecution?

5.44   The CPS will have had the opportunity to take over the private prosecution and discontinue it, on the ground that, given the weakness of the evidence, this is what the public interest requires. If it chooses not to do so, arguably it should take the consequences of the private prosecution's failure.[27] But it may be unrealistic to expect the CPS to discontinue a private prosecution *merely* because the case is not strong enough to justify a public one – particularly if the case has attracted publicity. Indeed, it is arguable that it may actually be in the public interest for a private prosecution to be allowed to take its course, albeit on evidence that would not pass the test laid down by the Code for Crown Prosecutors.[28] In the light of these considerations it may be arguable that a failure by the CPS to discontinue a doomed private prosecution should not have the same consequences as the failure of a public prosecution on the same evidence.

5.45   On the other hand, we have argued that the rule against double jeopardy is best justified on the basis of the distress which a retrial is likely to cause. From the defendant's point of view it may not make much difference whether the prosecution is public or private: the point is that the defendant is likely to be punished if convicted. The argument for treating an unsuccessful private prosecution in the same way as an unsuccessful public one is at its strongest where the case is *nearly* strong enough for the CPS to prosecute it, and in such a case the defendant may not derive much comfort from the knowledge that an acquittal is marginally more likely than a conviction. In a case such as this, we think that the same criterion of evidential strength should apply for the purposes of determining whether a retrial should be permitted. And in that case it is not easy to see how an exception might be made for those cases in which, because the acquittal was a foregone conclusion, the private prosecution will not have caused the defendant much concern. **We invite views on whether the minimum level of evidential**

[27]   In our report Consents to Prosecution (1998) Law Com No 255, at para 7.9, we recommended that court clerks should be required to notify the CPS of all private prosecutions (except those brought by organisations licensed for the purpose by the DPP) so that the CPS can consider whether they should be discontinued.

[28]   In our report Consents to Prosecution (1998) Law Com No 255, at para 5.22, we suggested that a private prosecution may sometimes be justifiable even if there is no "realistic prospect of a conviction", eg if the private prosecutor is the victim of the offence and knows the defendant to be guilty.

strength required under the proposal at paragraph 5.42 above should be any lower where the previous prosecution was a private one.

Evidence not available for the first trial

5.46 Should the prosecution have to show that the evidence would not have been available at the first trial, even if they had investigated with all due diligence? It would be unfortunate if the proposed exception were to have an adverse effect on police efficiency. It is worth noting that although the Court of Appeal, Criminal Division can admit new evidence on appeal whenever it considers that to do so would be in the interests of justice, it must nevertheless have regard to whether or not it could have been obtained at the trial by the exercise of due diligence.[29] What is meant by "due diligence" can be left for the courts to determine.[30]

5.47 It is possible that evidence may become available in the sense that it was inadmissible at the time of the first trial, and the law is changed so as to make it admissible. For example, a hearsay statement implicating the defendant, previously inadmissible under the rule against hearsay, might become admissible following a relaxation of that rule.[31] In such a case there could obviously be no criticism of the prosecution's failure to adduce the evidence in the first trial. The situation is analogous to one where, at the time of the first trial, the prosecution was aware of the existence of strong evidence, but was unable to find it; and in that case the exception for new evidence would clearly apply.

5.48 **We provisionally propose that**

   (1) **the power to reopen an acquittal on grounds of new evidence should be available only where that evidence could not, with due diligence, have been adduced at the first trial; but**

   (2) **evidence which was not admissible in the first trial, and subsequently becomes admissible owing to a change in the law, should count as new evidence.**

The interests of justice

5.49 One element of our hypothetical strongest case was that double jeopardy was the *only* reason why a retrial might be contrary to the interests of justice. That there should be an independent criterion in terms of the interests of justice seems to us to be clear. It is quite possible that there could be circumstances in which the evidence-related criteria are satisfied, but in which the defendant could not be fairly tried. One such case would be where, if it were a trial at first instance, an

---

[29] Criminal Appeal Act 1968, s 23.

[30] We note, for instance, that the test of whether "the prosecution has acted with all due expedition" in connection with custody time limits (Prosecution of Offences Act 1985, s 22(3)(b)) is that "the court must require such diligence and expedition as would be shown by a competent prosecutor conscious of his duty": *R v Manchester Crown Court, ex p McDonald* [1999] 1 WLR 841, 847.

[31] In our report Evidence in Criminal Proceedings: Hearsay and Related Topics (1997) Law Com No 245 we recommended a number of ways in which the rule might be relaxed.

application would be made for the indictment to be stayed as an abuse of process for some reason other than considerations of double jeopardy. For instance, there might have been so much prejudicial publicity that a fair trial would be impossible. It would at the very least be wasteful, and would inflict unnecessary distress on the defendant, to require him or her to make such an application to the judge presiding over the new trial, rather than at the stage at which the acquittal is quashed.

5.50 This conclusion is supported by Article 6 of the ECHR, which in effect requires that an accused person should not be deprived of the means of an effective defence. It is not difficult to envisage circumstances in which the defendant's ability to mount a defence in a second trial could be seriously undermined by the unusual course that the proceedings had taken. In our view, this requirement suggests that any power to allow a prosecution to be reopened on grounds of new evidence should be subject to a requirement that to do so would not be contrary to the interests of justice.[32]

5.51 Determining the interests of justice involves balancing the public interest in the prosecution of the guilty against that in fairness to the defendant. We think it should be made clear that the onus is on the prosecution to show that the former clearly outweighs the latter. **We provisionally propose that a retrial should be allowed on grounds of new evidence only where the court is satisfied that, in all the circumstances of the case, this is in the interests of justice.**

A time limit

5.52 In discussing the argument that the need for finality makes it undesirable for an acquittal ever to be reopened, we pointed out that this argument would lose much of its force if the proposed exception to the double jeopardy rule were subject to a time limit. We must now consider whether a time limit would be desirable.

5.53 In dealing with this question, a preliminary point should be made: the longer the delay between the alleged commission of an offence and the time when it is sought to prosecute the alleged offender, the stronger the case for not allowing the prosecution to proceed. Where the proposed defendant has not previously been tried for the offence, it is well established that the lapse of time may make a fair trial impossible, and in that case the prosecution will be stayed as an abuse of process. Obviously this might equally be so where the defendant has previously been tried and acquitted, and it is sought to reopen the acquittal many years later. We have proposed that the court invited to quash the acquittal, in determining whether a retrial would be in the interests of justice, should not look at the element of double jeopardy in isolation but should consider all the circumstances of the case. The time that has elapsed since the acquittal would clearly be a relevant consideration: it might, for example, make a fair trial impossible, or render the element of double jeopardy particularly unacceptable. The court might well decline to quash the acquittal on such grounds. Thus there is no question of the lapse of time being treated as *irrelevant*. The question is whether the court

---

[32] As in the case of the tainted acquittal procedure: Criminal Procedure and Investigations Act 1996, s 55(2).

should even have the *opportunity* to hold that, despite the lapse of time, the interests of justice require a retrial.

5.54 Here too we must weigh the two conflicting interests: the public interest in the prosecution of those against whom there is strong evidence of serious crime, and defendants' legitimate interest in being able to put the past behind them. Provided that the defendant can have a fair trial, we do not believe that the public interest in a prosecution for serious crime is substantially weakened by the passage of time. In this context it is noteworthy that there is in general no limitation period on criminal offences. Whenever a crime remains unsolved, both the offender and any other suspects are permanently at risk of further evidence being found and of being prosecuted as a result. In this case the law regards the public interest as outweighing the uncertainty caused by the absence of a time limit. The question is whether, by contrast, the law should set a limit on this uncertainty where the defendant has been tried and acquitted.

5.55 It is arguable that the law should distinguish between a person who is suspected of an offence, but has never been prosecuted for it, and a person who has been tried and acquitted. The uncertainty suffered by the former may be just as great; but that is a necessary consequence of the public interest in the prosecution of crime, and of the practical reality that some crimes take a long time to solve. A person who has once been tried and acquitted, on the other hand, has in a sense *earned* some degree of security through undergoing the ordeal of a trial. We have argued that such a person should not necessarily be entitled to *absolute* security against the acquittal ever being reopened. It does not follow that it would be fair for such a person to be exposed to that possibility for the rest of his or her life. The need for finality is a powerful consideration, and it is arguable that there should always be a point at which an acquitted person can be certain that that is the end of the matter.

5.56 It is also arguable that Article 6 of the ECHR might have a bearing on this issue, since it guarantees that the hearing should take place "within a reasonable time". The period that must not be unreasonable is that between "charge" and "determination". As we have explained, Article 4(2) allows the reopening of the original prosecution, rather than a re-prosecution for the same offence.[33] But it does not follow that there would be a breach of Article 6 if an acquittal were reopened many years later, because the period between the acquittal and the reopening would not count towards the relevant period. Any unwarranted delay in embarking on the reopening procedure *once the new evidence had been discovered*, on the other hand, presumably *would* count for the purposes of Article 6, because that delay would be aggregated with the length of the original proceedings. The resulting impetus to expedition on the part of the authorities is, we suggest, a welcome feature of the application of Article 6. Indeed we suggest that Article 6 would impose a general duty on the prosecuting authority to act with particular expedition at every stage, once the new evidence becomes available.

---

[33] See para 3.30 above.

49

5.57   We make no proposal as to what an appropriate time limit might be, and we invite views. But clearly there is a range of reasonable choices. If the limit were set at less than (say) six months, it would scarcely ever be possible to invoke the exception; and if it were set at more than (say) ten years, there would be little point in having a time limit at all. **We invite views as to whether an application to quash an acquittal on the grounds of new evidence should have to be made within a fixed period after the acquittal, and, if so, what that period should be.**

Successive retrials

5.58   As we have explained, we believe that the power to quash an acquittal on grounds of new evidence should be invoked only in exceptional circumstances. We find it scarcely conceivable that it might be in the interests of justice to invoke this exception more than once against the same defendant in respect of the same alleged facts; and we believe that this possibility should be ruled out altogether.

5.59   It is more likely that there might be a good case for invoking the new evidence exception against a defendant who has already faced a retrial on some other ground – for example, because the jury at the first trial could not agree. In some cases this might be a reason for the conclusion that it would be unfair to order yet another trial. But this would depend on the circumstances of the particular case. Where a six-month trial has resulted in the jury failing to agree, and the defendant has been acquitted after another six-month trial, it might well be unfair to subject the defendant to yet another six-month trial because new evidence has emerged. But if the jury at the first trial had to be discharged at an early stage, the fact that the defendant had already faced one retrial might be of limited relevance. We therefore do not believe that there should be an absolute rule against quashing an acquittal at a retrial: in our view this should be a matter to be taken into account by the court in deciding whether a third trial would be in the interests of justice.

5.60   **We provisionally propose that**

   (1)   **the exception for new evidence should not be available where the acquittal was at a retrial which itself was held by virtue of that exception; but**

   (2)   **where the acquittal was at a retrial held on some other ground, this should be only one factor to be taken into account in determining whether another retrial would be in the interests of justice.**

THE APPROPRIATE PROCEDURE

The nature of the hearing

5.61   What is required in terms of procedure should be determined by the task the court is being asked to perform. Its central task in exercising this jurisdiction would be the assessment of the strength of the evidence – both that adduced in the first trial and that now available.[34] In most cases, this would require the calling and cross-examination of witnesses able to give or produce the new evidence, as

---

[34]   See paras 5.30 – 5.42 above.

well as consideration of the evidence from the first trial on the basis of transcripts or, if necessary, the calling of witnesses. Such a task would clearly require an oral hearing at which both sides appear and are legally represented. If it were a hearing of this nature, the ordinary rule that the defendant should be present would apply. These are likely to be requirements of Article 6 of the ECHR: in our view they are in any event either necessary or desirable features of a hearing designed to accomplish the necessary tasks.[35]

The appropriate court

5.62 Recommendation 38 of the Macpherson Report specifically refers to the possibility of the *Court of Appeal* being empowered to permit retrials. The other obvious alternative would be the High Court, which is charged with quashing the acquittal under the tainted acquittal procedure. The Court of Appeal, Criminal Division has to apply similar criteria where an appellant seeks leave to adduce new evidence under section 23 of the Criminal Appeal Act 1968. In the High Court, the tainted acquittal procedure requires a similar exercise, at least where an application under that procedure is heard in open court.[36] And, of course, Queen's Bench judges find facts both in the Court of Appeal, Criminal Division and in civil proceedings.

5.63 It appears, therefore, that either court would be equally qualified to conduct the procedure outlined above. The choice between the two may therefore be determined by the desirability of a right of appeal, to which we now turn.

A right of appeal

5.64 We think it desirable that there should be a right of appeal against the decision to allow a retrial. The alternative, namely for any error to be rectified by an appeal against any conviction resulting from the retrial, seems unsatisfactory. If there is an error at the stage at which the acquittal is quashed, it seems wrong to subject the defendant to the anxiety of a second trial before it is rectified. An appeal at the earlier stage would also avoid the waste of public funds on a retrial. One disadvantage of such a right of appeal would be that there would inevitably be some delay in the commencement of the retrial. However, the experience of appeals against rulings at preliminary hearings under section 35 of the Criminal Procedure and Investigations Act 1996 suggests that such delays can be minimised.[37]

5.65 Clearly the court to which the appeal should lie is the Court of Appeal, Criminal Division. Appeal to the House of Lords is and should be limited to points of law of general public importance – a jurisdiction so limited as not to offer potential defendants real protection against error.

---

[35] For a discussion of the applicability and requirements of Article 6 in the context of tainted acquittals, see paras 6.31 – 6.38 below.

[36] Rules of the Supreme Court, Order 116, rule 10(3): Rules of the Supreme Court (Amendment) 1998, SI 1998 No 1898.

[37] See Simon Davis, "Interlocutory Appeals" [1988] 1 *Archbold News* 6.

5.66 We propose this "interlocutory" appeal as an alternative to the raising of the same issue in an appeal against any conviction at the retrial. This reasoning would suggest that the prosecution should not be able to appeal against a refusal to authorise a retrial. But the precedent of the right of appeal against a ruling at a preliminary hearing suggests otherwise.

5.67 As a result of our conclusion on the desirability of a right of appeal, we conclude that the court to which application may be made for the reopening of an acquittal should be the High Court.

5.68 **We provisionally propose**

(1) **that the decision whether to allow a retrial on grounds of new evidence should, in the first instance, be taken by the High Court;**

(2) **that there should be a right of appeal against a decision of the High Court to allow a retrial on those grounds; and**

(3) **that that right of appeal should be to the Criminal Division of the Court of Appeal.**

We invite views as to whether the prosecution should have a right of appeal against a refusal to allow a retrial.

NEW EVIDENCE RELATING TO A DIFFERENT OFFENCE

5.69 The focus of this part has been on the retrial of a defendant for the *same* offence, that being the form of retrial which cannot at present be justified on the basis of new evidence. We have argued that the rule against double jeopardy should be extended to cases currently governed by the *Connelly* principle,[38] so that a second prosecution would be barred where it was based on the same or substantially the same facts, even if it was for a different offence. This in turn opens up the possibility of a retrial where the defendant was *convicted* in the first trial. Where a defendant is convicted, it is of course unlikely that the prosecution would contemplate further proceedings for the same offence;[39] but it might wish to bring proceedings for a different, more serious offence. An example is *Beedie*,[40] where the defendant was charged with manslaughter after pleading guilty to an offence under the Health and Safety at Work Act 1974 which arose out of the same incident. If, as we have proposed, there were to be an exception where new evidence of an offence emerges after the defendant has been acquitted of that offence, there should clearly be a similar exception where new evidence of one offence emerges after the defendant has been convicted of another, less serious

---

[38] See Part IV above.

[39] Except perhaps to secure a heavier sentence, in a case in which the procedure for referring unduly lenient sentences to the Court of Appeal under the Criminal Justice Act 1988, s 36 is not available – eg most cases where the conviction is for an offence triable either way. If the defendant is convicted but not sentenced at all, there is no bar to further proceedings: *Richards* [1993] AC 217. See para 9.20 below.

[40] [1997] 2 Cr App R 167; see para 2.22 above.

offence on the same or substantially the same facts. But how would our proposals need to be modified for this situation?[41]

5.70 In the first place it would clearly be inappropriate that the way should be opened for the second prosecution by *quashing* the verdict in the first. There will be no inconsistency between the case now advanced by the prosecution and the earlier verdict, and there is therefore no reason why that verdict should not stand.[42] What is required is simply a power to authorise a second prosecution, the rule against double jeopardy notwithstanding.

5.71 The other modification that seems necessary is in relation to the criterion of evidential strength.[43] This will apply to both a conviction and an acquittal at the first trial, where the prosecution seek in the second trial to charge a different offence. Since the defendant will not even have been charged in the first trial with the offence of which new evidence has emerged,[44] there can be no question of comparing the evidence now available with the evidence adduced at the first trial.[45] In this situation we think the right approach is to compare the evidence now available with the evidence (if any) of the offence for which it is now sought to bring proceedings that was in the possession of the prosecution at the time when the defendant was charged with the other offence, and when (had sufficient evidence been available) the prosecution might have chosen to charge the offence that it now seeks to charge.

5.72 **We provisionally propose that, where the defendant has previously been tried for an offence, and new evidence suggests that he or she is guilty of a second, different, offence arising out of the same or substantially the same facts,**

(1) **where the first trial resulted in a conviction, the High Court should have power to authorise a prosecution for the second offence;**

(2) **the High Court should generally exercise its power (to authorise a prosecution for the second offence or to quash the acquital for the first) subject to the same conditions that, had the defendant been acquitted of the second offence at the time when he or she was convicted of the first offence, would have governed the court's power to quash that acquittal; but**

---

[41] It is possible that the defendant may have been acquitted of the offence revealed by the new evidence *and* convicted, in the same proceedings, of a lesser offence on the same facts. But in that case our earlier proposals would apply, in relation to the acquittal of the more serious offence. The legislation would of course need to provide that, if the acquittal is quashed, the conviction does not bar subsequent proceedings either.

[42] Indeed, the conviction will be admissible (though not conclusive) evidence that the defendant committed the offence of which he or she was convicted: Police and Criminal Evidence Act 1984, s 74(3).

[43] See paras 5.30 – 5.42 above.

[44] See n 41 above.

[45] See paras 5.34 – 5.38 above.

(3)   for the requirement we propose at paragraph 5.38 above (namely that the new evidence must make the prosecution's case substantially stronger than it was at the first trial) should be substituted a requirement that the new evidence must substantially strengthen the evidence (if any) of the second offence that was in the possession of the prosecution at the time when the defendant was charged with the first offence.

PART VI
FUNDAMENTAL DEFECT IN THE FIRST TRIAL

6.1   In this part we consider the second category of reopening allowed by Article 4(2), namely where there was a "fundamental defect" in the previous proceedings. The nature of this enquiry is different from that in Part V above, in that English law already contains the core of a procedure to reopen an acquittal where there is a "fundamental defect" – namely the tainted acquittal procedure outlined in Part II above.[1]

6.2   First we explain our understanding of the nature of the exception permitted by Article 4(2), and of the tainted acquittal procedure. We then consider whether the existing law is right to allow reopening in these circumstances, and conclude that it is. We go on to discuss the scope of the exception and conclude that it should be extended to certain other cases, including those where no-one has been convicted of an "administration of justice" offence. We turn then to the procedure, and conclude that it should be reformed. In the first place, it would have to be changed as a consequence of extending the scope of the exception in the way we propose. Secondly, we believe that the standard procedure, at least, does not comply with Article 6 of the ECHR. We therefore propose an alternative procedure.

THE NATURE OF "FUNDAMENTAL DEFECT" AND TAINTED ACQUITTALS

6.3   As we have explained,[2] Article 4(2) applies to extraordinary rather than ordinary remedies. It is therefore to be contrasted with what, in a Continental system, would be an "ordinary" prosecution right of appeal. Such a right of appeal, if introduced in the English legal system, would allow the prosecution to appeal against such things as misdirections made by the judge in the summing up, or erroneous rulings on the admissibility of evidence. This sort of ordinary ground of appeal would, in the nature of things, be apparent at or shortly after the conclusion of the trial. As a part of the ordinary proceedings, an appeal would be subject to a time limit.

6.4   A "fundamental defect", on the other hand, is extraordinary, and is likely to become apparent only after the acquittal is res judicata. We do not think it can apply to the sort of misdirections or errors which would be the subject of a prosecution right of appeal. Rather, it refers to a flaw in the trial which strikes at the foundations of the proceedings, and which one would ordinarily *not* expect to be evident immediately after the trial. If it were otherwise, we would expect the exception to conform to the model of a prosecution right of appeal, with the

---

[1]   We understand from the Head of the Crown Office that the procedure has yet to be used.

[2]   See para 3.28 above.

55

prosecution expected to make their objection within an appropriate, and reasonably short, time limit.[3]

6.5 Clearly, the subject matter of the tainted acquittal procedure fits this characterisation. We therefore regard the procedure as an existing exception to the autrefois rule which is permissible under Article 4(2) on grounds of "fundamental defect".

THE JUSTIFICATION FOR THE PROCEDURE

6.6 The tainted acquittal procedure is aimed at the defendant who benefits from an attack on the integrity of the criminal justice system itself, involving interference with, or intimidation of, a juror or witness. The interference or intimidation will itself be criminal, because it is a prerequisite of the procedure that an "administration of justice offence" should have been committed.[4] If it is the defendant who is responsible for the interference or intimidation, proceedings may be taken against the defendant for it, even if he or she is acquitted of the offence originally charged.[5] But it may not be the defendant who is responsible, or it may be impossible to prove this. Even if the defendant can be charged with the administration of justice offence, the original offence might be more serious. It is in principle objectionable that a defendant should escape conviction and punishment for the original offence because he or she has succeeded in interfering with or intimidating a juror or witness. We consider, therefore, that the tainted acquittal procedure is justifiable in principle.

THE SCOPE OF THE EXCEPTION

6.7 In this section, we consider whether the scope of the existing exception for tainted acquittals should be extended.

The objects of the interference or intimidation

6.8 The present procedure applies only where there has been interference with, or intimidation of, a *juror* or *witness*.[6] The thinking behind this restriction is presumably that the category should be strictly limited to those actors most closely involved in the trial process itself. We accept this argument. The procedure is an extraordinary one and should be reasonably closely confined. However, it would, on the same basis, be logical to include judges and magistrates. There is no evidence that interference with or intimidation of judges has hitherto been a problem, and we are not aware of any allegation that a magistrate has in recent

---

[3] The time limit for appealing against a conviction on indictment is 28 days: Criminal Appeal Act 1968, s 18(2).

[4] Criminal Procedure and Investigations Act 1996, s 54(1) and (6). The offences are perverting the course of justice, intimidation etc of witnesses, jurors and others (Criminal Justice and Public Order Act 1994, s 51(1)), and aiding, abetting, counselling, procuring, suborning or inciting another to commit perjury.

[5] And, if the defendant is convicted of the administration of justice offence, the tainted acquittal procedure would then be available: see *Hansard* (HL) 19 December 1995, vol 517, col 1583.

[6] Including a *potential* witness.

times been bribed or intimidated to secure an acquittal. But it would be complacent to assume that such an occurrence is inconceivable. **We provisionally propose that the tainted acquittal procedure should be extended so as to apply where the administration of justice offence involves interference with, or intimidation of, a judge or magistrate.**

The necessity for a conviction of an administration of justice offence

6.9 The present law requires that the person responsible for the intimidation or interference must be convicted of an administration of justice offence before the acquittal can be quashed.[7] It seems to us to be right that an acquittal can only be reopened when there is interference or intimidation amounting to an offence. That criterion establishes the seriousness of the interference or intimidation relied on, and ensures that it is directed at the criminal justice process. But we question the requirement that someone should have actually been *convicted* of such an offence. This requirement means that an acquittal could not be reopened if the author of the interference or intimidation were dead, or overseas, or had not been identified or apprehended. We believe that in such circumstances as these the exception should apply.

6.10 It would be possible to achieve this objective by discarding the requirement of a conviction altogether, and simply leaving it to the High Court in every case to determine whether it is satisfied (to the criminal standard of proof) that an administration of justice offence has been committed. This is our preferred solution. We do not consider that the High Court is necessarily a worse fact-finder than a jury; and, unless there is some particular virtue in the decision of a jury, this reform would make the procedure much easier to use without being unfair to either the person accused of the administration of justice offence or the acquitted person.

6.11 Alternatively, if it were thought that the requirement of a conviction serves a useful purpose, it could be retained subject to an exception for the case where it is impossible to try the person alleged to have committed the administration of justice offence. In such a case, the High Court would have to be satisfied (to the criminal standard of proof) that an administration of justice offence had in fact been convicted. Whether it was impossible to try the person allegedly responsible for the offence could be left at large for the High Court to decide, or there could be a list of allowable reasons (that the person could not be found, was abroad and not susceptible to extradition, was dead and so forth).

6.12 **We invite views on whether the requirement that a person should have been convicted of an administration of justice offence should be**

   (1) **retained in all cases;**

   (2) **abolished and replaced with a requirement that the High Court should be satisfied (to the criminal standard of proof) that an administration of justice offence has been committed; or**

---

[7] Criminal Procedure and Investigations Act 1996, s 54(3).

(3)   **retained except where it is impossible to try the person alleged to be guilty of the administration of justice offence, in which case the High Court should have to be satisfied (to the criminal standard of proof) that the offence has been committed.**

We provisionally propose the second option.

6.13   Were the second or the third option to be adopted, it is possible that a person might be prosecuted for the administration of justice offence after the High Court had found that the offence had been committed. While it would not be strictly necessary for the High Court to determine *who* had committed the offence, the disclosure of such a finding in a later trial for that offence would clearly be prejudicial. Evidence of that finding would probably be inadmissible in any event, but we think that it would be desirable to make this clear. **We provisionally propose that, if the second or the third option in paragraph 6.12 above were adopted, the fact that the High Court has found that an administration of justice offence has been committed should not be admissible in any subsequent trial of a person for that offence or an offence arising out of the same or substantially the same facts as that offence.**

The requirement that the acquittal be secured by the interference or intimidation

6.14   The separate requirement of a causal relationship between the interference or intimidation and the acquittal would remain. Misconduct which had no bearing on the acquittal does not call the acquittal into question. In the current procedure, the test is that it "appears to the High Court likely that, but for the interference or intimidation, the acquitted person would not have been acquitted".[8] The word "likely" can denote a range of probabilities. It has been said that it is to be construed in the context of the statute in which it appears, but widely differing answers have been given. Lord Diplock said "This word is imprecise. It is capable of covering a whole range of possibilities from 'it's on the cards' to 'it's more probable than not'".[9] In the context of the criminal statute he was considering,[10] it was to be understood as excluding only that which could fairly be described as highly unlikely. In another case concerning the same provision, the Court of Appeal accepted that it extended beyond probability to include something which could well happen.[11]

6.15   It may be that the lack of precision in the word "likely" is not problematic. On the other hand, it is arguable that the required *degree* of likelihood should be clear. One option would be to require proof to the civil standard – that it is *more probable*

---

8   Criminal Procedure and Investigations Act 1996, s 55(1).

9   *Shepherd* [1981] AC 394, 405.

10   Children and Young Persons Act 1933, s 1.

11   *Wills* [1990] Crim LR 714. Other cases in which "likely" is discussed include *Czarnikow v Koufos (The Heron II)* [1969] 1 AC 350, esp 390C-E, 410F-411A, 424G-425A; *Smith v Ainger, The Times* 5 June 1990; *Re S C L Building Services* (1989) 5 BCC 746; *Re Primlaks (UK)* [1989] BCLC 734.

than not that, but for the interference or intimidation, the defendant would not have been acquitted. Should the required likelihood be higher still? On one view, the level of probability should reflect the criminal standard: the High Court should satisfy itself so that it is *sure* that, but for the interference or intimidation, the acquitted person would not have been acquitted. But that might be an impossible demand. There will often be a real possibility that the jury may have disregarded the evidence of an intimidated witness, or taken no notice of the arguments of a bribed juror. That possibility, though low, may nevertheless be just high enough to defeat the criminal standard of proof.

6.16 An alternative approach would be to adopt the terminology of the test used in the Court of Appeal, Criminal Division in deciding whether to quash a conviction. The High Court would ask itself whether it was "safe" to conclude that the acquittal was secured by the interference or intimidation. The advantage would be that this would replicate an existing jurisdiction. A disadvantage is that it could be seen as evading the issue. Logically the court must adopt the ordinary civil standard of proof, the criminal standard or somewhere between the two; and the use of another form of words does not alter the necessity of making the choice.[12]

6.17 **We invite views on whether, when considering whether the acquittal was secured by the proven interference or intimidation, the High Court should apply**

   (1)   **the existing test (that this "appears to be likely");**

   (2)   **the civil standard of proof (that it is more likely than not);**

   (3)   **the criminal standard of proof (that the court is satisfied so that it is sure);**

   (4)   **the test applied by the Criminal Division of the Court of Appeal in deciding whether to quash a conviction on appeal (whether it is a "safe" conclusion); or**

   (5)   **some other test, and if so what.**

The definition of "administration of justice offence"

6.18 The administration of justice offences are perverting the course of justice; intimidating a witness or juror;[13] and aiding, abetting, counselling, procuring, suborning or inciting perjury.[14]

6.19 The question arises whether perjury itself, as distinct from being a secondary party to perjury, should be included. An amendment to that effect was moved by

---

[12]   It might be noted that the true construction of the "unsafe" test in Criminal Appeal Act 1968, s 2 has been a vexed issue within the court: see *Chalkley* [1998] QB 848, *Mullen v Conoco Ltd* [1998] QB 382.

[13]   Criminal Justice and Public Order Act 1994, s 51(1).

[14]   Perjury Act 1911, s 1.

Lord Ackner during the legislation's passage through Parliament, but was rejected by the Government.[15] We do not think it would be right to include perjury. The trial process itself is designed to determine which witnesses are telling the truth and which are lying. To lie in court is to do something which the trial process itself anticipates and tests. Secretly persuading, bribing or intimidating an apparently credible witness into lying, or not giving evidence at all, is not something the trial process is designed to deal with. Rather, it amounts to the kind of attack on *the process itself* that the tainted acquittal procedure is there to combat.

6.20   One way of testing the point is to ask what new material has been discovered to justify reopening the acquittal. The tainted acquittal procedure is established to deal with the discovery of bribery, intimidation or some similar interference with the administration of justice. In the absence of the discovery of anything new of that sort, an attempt to reopen an acquittal on the basis that the defence witnesses (perhaps including the defendant) were not telling the truth would amount to a simple refusal to accept the verdict. If there were a *new discovery*, on the other hand, which, without exposing any covert attack on the trial process, simply revealed that a defence witness had lied, it would amount to new evidence of the offence originally charged, and would be more appropriately dealt with under the exception for new evidence that we have proposed.[16]

6.21   **We invite views on whether, and if so how, the definition of an "administration of justice offence" should be extended.**

The interests of justice test

6.22   At present, the High Court may quash the acquittal only if it does not appear to be contrary to the interests of justice to do so. Our discussion of this criterion in Part V above[17] is equally relevant to the tainted acquittal procedure. Therefore, **we provisionally propose that the interests of justice test be formulated in the same way as we have proposed in the case of new evidence.**

Additional safeguards

6.23   When we considered whether the double jeopardy rule should be subject to an exception for new evidence, we concluded that there was a need for

(1)   a requirement that the offence now alleged should be of a certain minimum seriousness;

(2)   a stipulation that an acquittal could only be quashed once under this exception; and

(3)   arguably, a time limit, to render finite the period during which an acquitted defendant need fear that his or her acquittal might be reopened.

---

[15]   Hansard (HL) 19 December 1995, vol 567, cols 1580-1583.

[16]   See Part V above.

[17]   Paras 5.49 – 5.51.

6.24 The justifications for the double jeopardy rule are the same regardless of the possible exception under discussion, and it is arguable that these additional safeguards are as desirable in the case of the tainted acquittal procedure as they are in the context of new evidence. **We invite views on whether the tainted acquittal procedure should be subject to a seriousness criterion, a limit to the number of times the procedure may be used, or a time limit.**

THE PROCEDURE

6.25 The tainted acquittal jurisdiction is established in primary legislation, but the procedure, in both the Crown Court and the High Court, is very largely left to two sets of rules.[18] If our proposal to abolish the need for a conviction[19] were accepted, clearly there would be no Crown Court procedure at all. The need to find as a fact, on the criminal standard of proof, that an administration of justice offence had been convicted would place a greater burden on the High Court.

6.26 In the current procedure, the role of the High Court is to quash the acquittal, following the issuing of a certificate by the Crown Court under section 54(2), if the relevant conditions are met.[20] The subordinate legislation introduces two possible procedures. The standard procedure is for the judge to consider the making of the order to quash the acquittal in chambers on the basis of affidavits[21] alone, in the absence of the "acquitted person",[22] the prosecutor or any deponent.[23] There is also provision, however, for the judge to order a hearing in open court, on his or her own motion or on the application of the prosecutor or the acquitted person. The rules give the judge a power to order that a deponent attend for cross-examination.[24]

6.27 We consider that the standard procedure is not appropriate; or, at least, that it would cease to be appropriate if, as we propose, the requirement of a *conviction* for the administration of justice offence were abolished.[25] There are two reasons for

---

[18] The Crown Court (Criminal Procedure and Investigations Act 1996) (Tainted Acquittals) Rules 1997 (SI 1997 No 1054); Rules of the Supreme Court (Amendment) 1998 (SI 1998 No 1898), which introduces RSC O 116 in respect of the High Court.

[19] See para 6.12 above.

[20] The four conditions set out in s 55(1)–(4).

[21] The prosecutor's application (r 5) is to be accompanied by an affidavit which "deals with" condition 1 (the likelihood of an acquittal if there had been no interference or intimidation), condition 2 (that to take proceedings against the acquitted person is in the interests of justice) and condition 4 (that the conviction of the person responsible for the interference or intimidation will stand). The acquitted person has the opportunity to respond with an affidavit dealing with the same conditions (r 8), and there is procedure for the prosecutor, with leave, to file a further affidavit (r 9(2)–(4)). The affidavits may exhibit "any relevant documents", including a record of court proceedings (a transcript of a trial on indictment or the clerk's note in a summary trial: r 2), and it is presumably by reference to this record of both the original trial of the acquitted person and the trial for the administration of justice offence that the first condition would be proved.

[22] The person whose acquittal the prosecution seek to quash: (r 2).

[23] RSC O 116 r 3, r 10(1).

[24] Rule 10(3)–(13).

[25] See para 6.12 above.

this. The first is that it appears to us to constitute an unjustified departure from the usual rule in English law that substantive issues are judicially determined after an oral hearing. The second is that it does not comply with Article 6 of the ECHR. We consider each argument in turn.

The absence of an oral hearing

6.28 The general rule is that substantive questions are determined in a public adversarial oral hearing. The same is not necessarily true of interlocutory matters or leave requirements. It seems to us that the tainted acquittal procedure is more properly seen as determining the substantive question of whether the acquittal should be quashed, rather than as a mere preliminary or leave stage in respect of the retrial. Typically, leave procedures scrutinise the case put forward by the party initiating the proceedings with a view to stopping it going any further if it is of so little merit that it is bound not to succeed. They exist to winnow out unarguable cases, thus saving courts (sitting in public and conducting adversarial, oral hearings) from wasting time on them. By contrast, the tainted acquittal procedure overturns a final judicial decision in favour of the acquitted person, to that person's potentially very considerable disadvantage. It is brought on the application of the Crown, not the acquitted person, and requires the court to adjudicate between the two competing positions.

6.29 It may be that, as the procedure is now designed, this criticism loses some force because of the role of the Crown Court. The High Court considers the quashing of the acquittal only after the Crown Court has tried and convicted a person for an administration of justice offence associated with the acquittal. But we propose that the Crown Court should cease to be involved.[26] Further, although it may seem reasonable that the present procedure is conducted essentially on the basis of the papers,[27] if our proposal were adopted, the High Court would have to be satisfied that an administration of justice offence had in fact been committed. We would ordinarily expect this process to require the calling and cross-examination of witnesses. In the context of the traditions of English law, such a fact-finding exercise could be properly undertaken only in a public hearing of this sort.

6.30 Accordingly, we consider that, at least if our proposal to discard the requirement of a Crown Court certificate is adopted, the procedure in the High Court should

---

[26] In any event, the role of the Crown Court is not without difficulties. The Crown Court is required to be satisfied that there is a "real possibility" that, but for the administration of justice offence, the acquitted person would not have been acquitted. But the evidence called by the Crown to prove the administration of justice offence would not necessarily go to suggest that causal connection. Indeed, evidence directed solely at that conclusion would normally be irrelevant and inadmissible in the trial for the administration of justice offence. No procedure is set down for the separate proof of the causal link, and the requirement in the rules that certification take place immediately after sentence would suggest that no such procedure is envisaged. Nor is the acquitted person represented (unless he or she is also the person convicted of the administration of justice offence).

[27] Although it is perhaps unfortunate that no express provision is made for *representations* (if only in writing) by the parties, in apparent contradiction to s 55(3). The only written instrument for which provision is made in the rules is an affidavit, which does not properly contain argument.

be conducted orally in open court, in the presence of the acquitted person, and with both the acquitted person and the Crown legally represented.

Article 6

6.31 This conclusion is reinforced by Article 6 of the ECHR. Article 6(1) entitles the defendant to "a fair and public hearing", and Article 6(3)(c) confers the right "to defend himself in person or through legal assistance of his own choosing".

The application of Article 6

6.32 There has been no decision of the Strasbourg Court that a court considering the reopening of a prosecution in accordance with Article 4(2) is bound by Article 6. Nevertheless, we believe that it would almost certainly so decide if the question arose, and that a domestic court considering the question (once the Human Rights Act 1998 is in force) should come to the same conclusion.

6.33 Article 6 imposes a requirement of a fair trial in "the determination of ... any criminal charge". A person whose acquittal the prosecution seeks to quash would not be "charged" with a criminal offence in the sense known to English law. However, the term "charge" in the Convention has an autonomous meaning in the Strasbourg jurisprudence.[28] It is to be given a substantive rather than a formal meaning. So, although it involves some official notification being given to the defendant that he or she has been accused of a criminal offence, it can be constituted by any official act that carries such an implication.[29] The test is whether the defendant is "substantially affected" by the official steps taken.[30] A wide range of official acts have been found to constitute a charge.[31]

6.34 Two further cases are of particular interest. In *Frau v Italy*,[32] the Court accepted as the time of charge a request to the Chamber of Deputies to remove the applicant's Parliamentary immunity. Such a request is the commencement of the determination of a pre-condition to the determination of the criminal charge itself, and may thus be seen as a parallel to the quashing of a previous acquittal.

---

[28] *Deweer v Belgium* A 35 (1980).

[29] *Corigliano v Italy* A 57 (1982).

[30] *Deweer v Belgium* A 35 (1980).

[31] "A person has been found to be subject to a 'charge' when arrested for a criminal offence; when officially informed of the prosecution against him; when, in a civil law system, a preliminary investigation has been opened in his case and, although not under arrest, the applicant has 'officially learnt of the investigation or begun to be affected by it'; when authorities investigating customs offences require a person to produce evidence and freeze his bank account; when his shop has been closed pending the payment of a sum by way of friendly settlement or the outcome of criminal proceedings that would be instituted if the sum were not paid; and when the applicant has appointed a defence lawyer after the opening of a file by the public prosecutor's office following a police report against him." Harris, O'Boyle and Warbrick, *Law of the European Convention on Human Rights* (1995) pp 171–172 (footnotes omitted).

[32] A 195-E (1991).

6.35   More directly relevant is *Callaghan v UK*, in which the Commission concluded that Article 6 did apply where a case was referred to the Court of Appeal, Criminal Division by the Home Secretary under section 17 of the Criminal Appeal Act 1968 (before its amendment by the Criminal Appeal Act 1995). The Commission recognised that the procedure was not part of the ordinary appeal process and took place long after the completion of the criminal proceedings by an ordinary appeal. Nevertheless,

> the proceedings on the Secretary of State's reference had all the features of an appeal against conviction, and could have resulted in the applicants being found not guilty or ... the convictions being upheld. They must therefore in the Commission's view be regarded as having the effect of determining, or re-determining, the charges against the applicants.[33]

6.36   Similar considerations would seem to apply to any hearing of an application to reopen an acquittal where this is allowed by Article 4(2), and we conclude that Article 6 would apply to it. Given our conclusion that the tainted acquittal procedure *is* such a procedure, it follows that Article 6 applies to that.[34] The official act constituting a "criminal charge" would presumably be the notice that the prosecution is required to give the defendant of its application to have the acquittal quashed.[35]

The requirements of Article 6

6.37   If Article 6 applies, the standard procedure clearly does not comply with it. As a general rule Article 6(1) and Article 6(3)(c), taken together, require that an accused person should be entitled to be present, and to be legally represented, in any appellate proceedings. The Strasbourg Court has consistently held that Article 6 implies the right of an accused person to participate effectively in criminal proceedings,[36] and has held that it is "of crucial importance for the fairness of the criminal justice system that the accused be adequately defended, both at first instance and on appeal".[37] These requirements must, in our view, apply equally to proceedings brought with a view to the reopening of an acquittal, where this is permitted by Article 4(2).

6.38   It is true that the applicability of particular elements of the Article 6 guarantees may vary according to the nature of the proceedings. So, for instance, although the article applies to ordinary proceedings on appeal, the presumption of innocence

---

[33]   (1989) 60 DR 296.

[34]   Because we provisionally propose the abolition of certification at the Crown Court, we do not consider the difficult question of whether Article 6 applies to this stage.

[35]   Under RSC O 116, r 6.

[36]   See, eg, *Ekbatani v Sweden* A 134 (1988) at paras 25–33.

[37]   *Lala v Netherlands* A 247-A (1994) at para 33. See also *Pelladoah v Netherlands* A 297-B (1994) at para 40.

guaranteed in Article 6(2) does not.[38] In *Ekbatani v Sweden*[39] the Court pointed out that the application of Article 6 to appellate proceedings depends upon the special features of the proceedings involved. In determining whether an inter partes oral hearing is required, account should be taken of the nature of the domestic proceedings, and the functions of the appellate court within those proceedings. But, where the appellate court is called upon to examine the facts of a case, and to make an assessment of the probative weight of evidence adduced by the prosecution, an adversarial oral hearing will generally be required.

6.39 That is not to say that *all* of the Article 6 guarantees are applicable to the tainted acquittal procedure. Article 6(3)(d) guarantees a right to call witnesses on the same basis as the prosecution. But the tainted acquittal procedure is engaged (in part) in determining what *would* have happened at the acquitted person's trial in the absence of interference or intimidation. It therefore seems right and appropriate to proceed, as the current procedure provides, by reference to transcripts of the trial, rather than allow witnesses to be called on that question. On the other hand, we would expect witnesses to be required on the quite separate factual issue of whether an administration of justice offence has been committed. In deciding *this* issue, the evidence should prima facie be produced "in the presence of the accused at a public hearing with a view to adversarial argument".[40]

The alternative existing procedure and Article 6

6.40 In the context of the existing procedure it should be noted that, one element apart, the alternative procedure under rule 10(3) appears to be compliant with Article 6, bearing in mind the qualified nature of the right to call witnesses.[41] The one problem is that under rule 9(2) only the prosecutor can apply for leave to file further affidavit evidence. This offends against the principle of equality of arms. However, no doubt the court could, in its inherent jurisdiction, make provision for the acquitted person to be treated equally. In practice, therefore, the procedure could be *operated* in a compliant way. Until the Human Rights Act 1998 comes into force, the alternative procedure could therefore be used to ensure that the proceedings are compliant with Article 6. Once the Act is in force, the standard procedure (being a creature of subordinate legislation, and non-compliant) would

---

[38] *Delcourt v Belgium* A 11 (1970), *Callaghan v UK* (1989) 60 DR 296. Similarly, the distinction between an application for leave and a substantive hearing is reflected in what Article 6 requires. In *Monnell and Morris v UK* A 115 (1987) the Court found that Article 6 did not require an oral hearing or the presence of the defendants on the hearing by a single judge of their applications for leave to appeal against conviction, nor their presence or representation at a renewed application before the full Court of Appeal, Criminal Division. On the other hand, in the Scottish cases of *Granger v UK* A 174 (1990), *Boner v UK* A 300-B (1994) and *Maxwell v UK* A 300-C (1994) the Court found that a failure to provide free representation where there was a *right* of appeal was a violation. For cases in which the Commission has found that Article 6 did not even apply to leave applications, see P van Dijk and G J H van Hoof, *Theory and Practice of the European Convention on Human Rights* (3rd ed 1998) p 423.

[39] A 134 (1988) at paras 25–33.

[40] *Barberà, Messegué and Jabardo v Spain* A 146 (1988) para 78.

[41] See para 6.39 above.

presumably be declared void by any court considering it,[42] and only the alternative procedure would be available.

Proposals on the procedure

6.41   **We provisionally propose that provision be made**

> (1)   **for a hearing of the question whether the acquittal should be quashed;**
>
> (2)   **for the hearing to be in open court;**
>
> (3)   **for the acquitted person to have a right to be present;**
>
> (4)   **for both parties to be legally represented, and legal aid to be available for the acquitted person;**
>
> (5)   **for witnesses to be heard and cross-examined on the question whether an administration of justice offence has been committed; and**
>
> (6)   **for consideration of transcripts of the first trial, together with witnesses if necessary, in determining whether the acquitted person would not have been acquitted but for the interference or intimidation.**

---

[42]   Human Rights Act 1998, s 3. The only reference to the nature of the procedure in the primary legislation is s 55(3), which makes it a condition of the issuing of an order that the acquitted person has had a reasonable opportunity to make representations in writing. But this could hardly be sufficient to make the standard procedure fall into the category of subordinate legislation that is required to be non-compliant by its parent primary legislation (Human Rights Act 1998, s 3(2)(c)).

PART VII
THE ROLE OF JUDICIAL DISCRETION

7.1 In this part we discuss how far it should be possible, under the new regime we propose, for a court to exercise a discretion to stay a prosecution on grounds of double jeopardy. At present, judicial discretion arises chiefly where the defendant has previously been acquitted or convicted of an offence which was not the offence now charged, but which arose out of the same or substantially the same facts as that offence. In these circumstances, under the *Connelly* principle,[1] there is no absolute bar to a prosecution, and the court has a discretion to allow the case to proceed if there are special circumstances which justify this.

7.2 Moreover, if this discretion is separate from the discretion to stay proceedings on grounds of abuse of process,[2] the latter discretion must in theory be available too. This overlap is of no significance under the present law, because in an abuse of process application the burden is on the defence to show why the case should not proceed, whereas in a double jeopardy case the burden is on the prosecution to show why it should. If the defence can discharge the former burden then, a fortiori, the prosecution will not be able to discharge the latter. But we must consider both kinds of discretion, because, on the assumption that they are distinct, if only one of them were excluded the other would presumably continue to be available.

THE *CONNELLY* PRINCIPLE

7.3 We proposed in Part IV that the autrefois rule should be extended so as to apply not only (as at present) where the defendant is charged with the same offence as before, but also where he or she is charged with a different offence on the same or substantially the same facts. The new rule against double jeopardy would thus swallow up those cases where at present the *Connelly* principle applies.

7.4 Where the *Connelly* principle applies, the court has a discretion to allow the second prosecution if there are special circumstances which justify this. It would be possible to retain this discretion, as an exception to the (extended) rule against double jeopardy, and indeed to extend it to cases where at present a retrial is completely prohibited under the autrefois rule. Such an exception would make it unnecessary to have specific exceptions for tainted acquittals or new evidence. But it would make for great uncertainty if the courts had an unfettered discretion to allow double jeopardy whenever they think it would be in the interests of justice. Moreover, under the Human Rights Act 1998 it would be unlawful for a court to exercise such a discretion, at any rate in a case which now falls within the autrefois rule, in circumstances other than those where a reopening of the case is permitted by Article 4(2); and this might also be unlawful in a case which now falls outside the autrefois rule but is subject to the *Connelly* principle.[3] If the courts could not

---

[1] See para 2.21 above.

[2] As appears to have been the view of the court that decided *Beedie* [1998] QB 356.

[3] This would depend whether the wider interpretation of Article 4(1) in *Gradinger v Austria* A 328-C (1995) prevails over the narrower interpretation adopted in *Oliveira v Switzerland* 1998-V p 1990: see paras 3.19 – 3.27 above.

lawfully exercise a discretion wider than Article 4 permits, there is no advantage, and some disadvantage, in purporting to give them such a discretion.

7.5 **We provisionally propose that the *Connelly* principle should be wholly superseded by the extended rule against double jeopardy.** This means that, where an exception to the rule applies, the defence would not be able to invoke the *Connelly* principle. Conversely, where *no* exception applies, the prosecution would not be able to circumvent the rule by arguing that there are "special circumstances" which fall within no recognised exception. Any case of double jeopardy would *either* be prohibited under the new rule *or* permitted under a specific exception to the new rule.

ABUSE OF PROCESS

7.6 The doctrine of abuse of process, unlike the *Connelly* principle, applies in many cases which do not involve double jeopardy at all, and must obviously be retained alongside the new rule. But one form of abuse of process is the situation where it is unfair to put the defendant on trial at all, and double jeopardy is generally thought to be one such situation. Thus, where double jeopardy would otherwise be permitted under an exception to the rule, the defence might invite the court to exercise a residual discretion to stay the proceedings; and, if the discretion conferred by the *Connelly* principle were to disappear as we have proposed, the defence might fall back on the argument that the proceedings are an abuse of process. Arguably this should be prevented, since, under our proposals, an acquittal could not be quashed without the High Court considering all the circumstances of the case, and satisfying itself that a retrial would be in the interests of justice.[4] If an acquittal were nevertheless quashed, an application for the retrial to be stayed might involve a rehearing of arguments that had already been heard and rejected.

7.7 It would be possible to avoid such an outcome by providing that, where an acquittal is quashed under one of the exceptions to the rule against double jeopardy, there can be no application for the ensuing retrial to be stayed as an abuse of process unless there has been a material change of circumstances since the acquittal was quashed. But our provisional view is that there is no need for a rule to this effect. If the defence were able to apply for the proceedings to be stayed, the court hearing such an application would in practice give proper weight to the previous decision to quash the acquittal. Where the High Court has ruled that it is in the interests of justice for the defendant to be tried again, the trial judge is unlikely to take a different view unless there has been a material change of circumstances; and, if an abuse of process application simply rehearses the same arguments as have already failed in a higher court, it will be quickly disposed of.

7.8 **We provisionally propose that a person whose acquittal is quashed under an exception to the rule against double jeopardy should not be precluded from applying for further proceedings to be stayed as an abuse of process.**

---

[4] See paras 5.51 and 6.22 above.

PART VIII
THE RULE AGAINST CHALLENGING A PREVIOUS ACQUITTAL

8.1 In this part we consider what, if anything, should be done about the rule in *Sambasivam*,[1] which states that an acquittal cannot subsequently be challenged in other proceedings against the same defendant by adducing evidence that he or she was in fact guilty of the offence of which he or she was acquitted. First we examine the present scope and effect of the rule, and the basis for it. We then consider whether it serves a useful purpose as a further safeguard against double jeopardy, and provisionally conclude that it does not. Finally we consider whether it has any useful role outside the sphere of double jeopardy, as a kind of issue estoppel; and again we provisionally conclude that it does not. We therefore provisionally propose that it be abolished.

THE RULE

8.2 In *Sambasivam* the accused was originally charged on two counts of possessing a firearm and possessing ammunition. It was alleged that he had made a statement which was a confession to both charges; he denied making this statement. He was acquitted on the ammunition charge, but the firearm charge had to be retried. At the retrial the confession was adduced in evidence, without reference to the acquittal, and the accused was convicted. The Privy Council held that this conviction should be set aside because it had not been made clear that, as regards the ammunition offence, the confession must be taken to be untrue. Lord MacDermott said:

> The effect of a verdict of acquittal pronounced by a competent court on a lawful charge and after a lawful trial is not completely stated by saying that the person acquitted cannot be tried again for the same offence. To that it must be added that the verdict is binding and conclusive in all subsequent proceedings between the parties to the adjudication. The maxim "Res judicata pro veritate accipitur"[2] is no less applicable to criminal than to civil proceedings.[3]

8.3 A similar conclusion was reached in *G v Coltart*.[4] The defendant, a servant, was charged with larceny of property belonging to her employer and, separately, larceny of property belonging to a guest. The prosecution offered no evidence on the charge relating to the guest, because she was not available to testify, but relied on the circumstances in which her property was found in the defendant's room as rebutting the defendant's claim that she had intended to give all the property

---

[1] *Sambasivam v Public Prosecutor, Federation of Malaya* [1950] AC 458.

[2] A thing adjudicated is received as truth: *Osborn's Concise Law Dictionary* (8th ed 1993).

[3] [1950] AC 458, 479.

[4] [1967] 1 QB 432.

back. On appeal her conviction was quashed. The court was not referred to *Sambasivam* and made no reference to it, but Salmon LJ held that

> on general principles ... it would be quite wrong to allow the prosecution in order to obtain a conviction in case B to seek to show that the defendant was guilty in case A, after the defendant has been acquitted in case A.[5]

8.4 *Sambasivam* was applied in *Hay*.[6] The defendant signed a confession relating to charges of arson and burglary. He was tried first with arson, and an edited confession, removing all reference to the burglary, was put before the jury. He was acquitted after arguing that he had been tricked into signing the confession. He was then charged with burglary, and the *defence* insisted that the entire confession should go before the jury so that the previous acquittal could be relied upon to prove that at least some of the confession was false. The trial judge refused to allow this. On appeal, the conviction was quashed.

> The jury ought to have been told of the acquittal and directed that it was conclusive evidence that the appellant was not guilty of arson, and that his confession to that offence was untrue. The jury should also have been directed that in deciding the contest between the appellant and the police officers as to the part of the statement referring to the burglary, they should keep in mind the first part must be regarded as untrue.[7]

The case is similar to *Sambasivam*,[8] in that it was held that the confession must be taken to be untrue in so far as it related to the offence of which the defendant had been acquitted. It made no difference that it was the defence, rather than the prosecution, who sought to adduce it.

8.5 The rule is not easy to reconcile with *DPP v Humphrys*,[9] where the House of Lords held that there is no issue estoppel in the criminal law. The defendant was stopped by a police officer for speeding and charged with riding a motor cycle whilst disqualified. He testified that it was a case of mistaken identity, as he had not ridden his motor cycle during the period of his disqualification, and was acquitted. Subsequent inquiries revealed that he *had* been riding his motor cycle whilst disqualified, and he was tried for perjury. The police officer repeated his evidence, which was clearly inconsistent with the previous acquittal, and

---

[5] [1967] 1 QB 432, 439G.

[6] (1983) 77 Cr App R 70.

[7] *Ibid*, p 75, *per* O'Connor LJ.

[8] In *H* (1990) 90 Cr App R 440, 444 it was said that *Hay* appeared to be "almost a re-run" of *Sambasivam*. The facts of *H* were somewhat similar to those of *Hay*, but this time it was held that the judge had been right to prevent the defence from relying on the previous acquittal. *Hay* was distinguished on the ground that the acquittal could only have been on the basis that the confession was fabricated, whereas in *H* there were other possible explanations. Evidence of the defendant's earlier acquittals would have distracted the jury from determining the truth on the facts before them, and deflected them into considering what had led the earlier jury to come to the conclusions it did.

[9] [1977] AC 1.

Humphrys was convicted. He appealed on the ground that, under the doctrine of issue estoppel, the issue of whether he was the rider stopped by the police officer had been finally settled in his favour. The House of Lords held that the doctrine of issue estoppel was confined to the civil law.[10] The officer's evidence was therefore admissible.

8.6 Even if the House of Lords was right to hold that there is no issue estoppel in criminal law, it is hard to see why the rule in *Sambasivam* did not lead to the same result. The application of that rule would have barred the prosecution from asserting that Humphrys was guilty of the charge on which he had been acquitted. *Sambasivam* was distinguished on the ground that the rule was concerned with the binding nature of a previous acquittal rather than with the determination of any particular issue at the previous trial. But this distinction is questionable. The police officer's evidence at the trial for perjury effectively contradicted the verdict at the previous trial, since the only issue in that trial was the rider's identity.[11]

8.7 The position is further complicated by the House of Lords' subsequent decision in *Hunter v Chief Constable of West Midlands*.[12] The plaintiff in that case had been convicted of murder after the trial judge found on a voir dire that his confession had not (as he alleged) been secured by violence on the part of the police, and was therefore admissible. He subsequently brought a civil action against the police for damages in respect of the alleged assaults. Lord Diplock, giving the only reasoned judgment, expressed a preference for confining the description "issue estoppel" to civil cases in accordance with *Humphrys*.[13] But he also held that it was immaterial whether the plaintiff was technically estopped from repeating the allegation rejected at his trial, because the action was in any event an abuse of process.

> The abuse of process which the instant case exemplifies is the initiation of proceedings in a court of justice for the purpose of mounting a collateral attack upon a final decision against the intending plaintiff which has been made by another court of competent jurisdiction in previous proceedings in which the intending plaintiff had a full opportunity of contesting the decision in the court by which it was made.[14]

8.8 In *Hunter* itself the decision the plaintiff sought to attack was a decision of a criminal court, but the proceedings through which he sought to attack it were

---

[10] There is a limited exception in the case of an application for habeas corpus: *Governor of Brixton Prison, ex p Osman* [1991] 1 WLR 281.

[11] See M Hirst, "Contradicting Previous Acquittals" [1991] Crim LR 510; *Andrews and Hirst on Criminal Evidence* (3rd ed 1997) p 761; P Mirfield, "Shedding a Tear for Issue Estoppel" [1980] Crim LR 336. Hirst states that counsel for Humphrys did not rely on the rule in *Sambasivam*, and suggests that the House of Lords might have adopted a different approach if he had: [1991] Crim LR 510, 518. But, although counsel put his argument in terms of issue estoppel, he argued that the rule in *Sambasivam* amounted to the same thing: [1977] AC 1, 7H (R J S Harvey QC).

[12] [1982] AC 529. The case concerned the Birmingham pub bombings of 1974.

[13] In *Humphrys* the House had adopted the formulation of the doctrine advanced by Diplock LJ (as he then was) in *Mills v Cooper* [1967] 2 QB 459, 468–469.

[14] [1982] AC 529, 541.

civil. In the recent case of *R v Belmarsh Magistrates' Court, ex p Watts*[15] the Divisional Court seems to have been willing to apply the same principle where *criminal* proceedings amount to a collateral attack. The case concerned a private prosecution against a Customs officer which was brought with a view to challenging the prosecutor's own conviction for importing drugs. But the same principle would presumably apply where the proceedings amount to a collateral attack on a previous acquittal of the defendant – for example, where the prosecution seeks to charge the defendant with perjury at the first trial, on the basis of the same evidence as before. Under the *Hunter* principle, such proceedings would be an abuse of process. The defendant can therefore be protected against such tactics without the need to invoke either issue estoppel or the rule in *Sambasivam*. The importance of *Sambasivam* seems to lie in the case where the proceedings as a whole do not amount to an abuse of process (because a conviction on the second charge would not necessarily controvert the acquittal on the first), but the prosecution seeks to adduce *evidence* which, if accepted, shows the acquittal to have been wrong.

THE BASIS OF THE RULE

8.9   The basis of the rule in *Sambasivam* is a source of disagreement. It has sometimes been described as an extension of the rule against double jeopardy.[16] Others have argued that it is a separate rule, more closely related to that of issue estoppel.[17]

8.10   We see some force in the first view. The rule does protect a defendant who has been acquitted of an offence from being prosecuted again for the same offence, or for a different offence based on the same facts. But in that case the defendant is also protected by the rule against double jeopardy.[18] Indeed, it is the overlap with that rule that has led us to deal with the *Sambasivam* rule in this paper. But these rules are not co-extensive, and neither is subsumed within the other. Where the defendant has previously been *convicted* on the same facts, there is no question of that decision being challenged by a subsequent prosecution, and the rule in *Sambasivam* therefore does not apply. Conversely, even if the defendant has previously been acquitted in respect of facts now *alleged*, the rule against double jeopardy has no application if the *charge* is based on different facts – for example, if the new charge relates to the defendant's conduct on a different occasion from the first, but the prosecution seeks to rely on the defendant's guilt on the first occasion as "similar fact" evidence in relation to the second.

8.11   In the context of this paper, therefore, the rule has two aspects, which we consider in turn. The first is its application to a case of true double jeopardy – that is, the situation where a person is prosecuted for a second time on the same or

---

[15]   [1999] 2 Cr App R 188.

[16]   Eg, by Lord Devlin in *Connelly* [1964] AC 1254 at p 1341, by Diplock LJ in *Mills v Cooper* [1967] 2 QB 459 at p 496D, and by Lord Hailsham LC in *Humphrys* [1977] AC 1 at p 37E.

[17]   See P Mirfield, "Shedding a Tear for Issue Estoppel" [1980] Crim LR 336, M Hirst, "Contradicting Previous Acquittals" [1991] Crim LR 510 and *Andrews and Hirst on Criminal Evidence* (3rd ed 1997) p 761. While Mirfield goes on to argue that issue estoppel should be extended, Hirst's view is that the rule in *Sambasivam* should be abolished.

[18]   That is, the combination of autrefois acquit and the *Connelly* principle: see para 2.21 above.

substantially the same facts, having already been once acquitted. The second and more difficult issue is whether the rule should continue to apply in cases where, although the prosecution's evidence contradicts the previous acquittal, the charge itself does not amount to double jeopardy, and there is therefore no need to get the acquittal quashed before proceeding with the second charge. This latter situation is, by definition, not a case of double jeopardy, and it is considered in this paper only because it is not easy to disentangle this aspect of the rule from its function in relation to double jeopardy.

8.12 In effect, and despite the House of Lords' insistence in *Humphrys* that there is no issue estoppel in criminal law, in its application to cases not involving double jeopardy the rule seems to work as a kind of issue estoppel. But it is a curious and limited kind of estoppel, in two ways. First, it only works against the prosecution, not the defence.[19] Second, it only works in relation to an issue which has been conclusively decided against the prosecution. Because juries do not give reasons for their verdicts, it will often be the case that the only issue conclusively decided by an acquittal is the defendant's innocence of the charge. Usually, therefore, that will be the *only* issue which the prosecution cannot reopen. It may be able to repeat the individual allegations made at the first trial, if it is not clear which of those allegations were rejected by the fact-finders. What it cannot do, according to *Sambasivam*, is to assert, as part of its case, that the defendant was in fact guilty as charged.

DOUBLE JEOPARDY CASES

8.13 We consider first the relationship between the rule in *Sambasivam* and the doctrine of autrefois acquit, and then the relationship between the rule in *Sambasivam* and the *Connelly* principle.

Sambasivam and autrefois acquit

8.14 Clearly the rule in *Sambasivam* overlaps with the doctrine of autrefois acquit. To the extent that our proposed rule against double jeopardy would replace that doctrine, there would be no harm in allowing the rule in *Sambasivam* to overlap with our proposed rule; but in those cases where the rule against double jeopardy prevented the prosecution from proceeding at all, the rule in *Sambasivam* would be redundant.

8.15 It would of course be necessary to ensure that the *exceptions* to the rule against double jeopardy were not undermined by the rule in *Sambasivam*. Where an acquittal is quashed under an exception to the former rule, thus enabling the defendant to be tried again for the same offence, the defence might argue that some or all of the prosecution evidence should be excluded under the rule in *Sambasivam*, because it contradicts the previous acquittal. But logically such an argument ought to fail, because once the previous acquittal has been quashed it no longer has any force. Whatever justification there might previously have been

---

[19] Where a defendant's conviction of an offence is admissible as proof that the defendant committed that offence, the defendant is permitted to adduce evidence that he or she was wrongly convicted: Police and Criminal Evidence Act 1984, s 74(3).

for excluding evidence that would contradict the acquittal, it can no longer apply. It is therefore most unlikely that, under the present law, the rule in *Sambasivam* could be invoked after an acquittal has been quashed under the tainted acquittal provisions;[20] and similarly we do not think it could be invoked where an acquittal was quashed under the exception that we propose for cases of new evidence.[21]

Sambasivam and the *Connelly* principle

8.16 The relationship between the rule in *Sambasivam* and the *Connelly* principle is obscure. In *Connelly*, as we have seen,[22] it was held that the court has a discretion to allow a prosecution to proceed although the defendant has previously been acquitted or convicted on the same or substantially the same facts, if the earlier charge was for a different offence. If the rule in *Sambasivam* applies, it follows that there is no such discretion where the defendant has already been *acquitted* in relation to those facts, and the second charge is inconsistent with that acquittal (as it usually will be).

8.17 The *Connelly* principle was reaffirmed in *Beedie*.[23] Neither *Sambasivam* nor *Humphrys* was cited, doubtless because in *Beedie* the defendant had previously been *convicted* on the facts that gave rise to the second charge.[24] But *Connelly* involved a previous acquittal. Connelly was acquitted of a murder which had been committed in the course of a robbery, and his subsequent conviction for participating in the robbery was upheld. Lord Devlin distinguished *Sambasivam* on the basis that the prosecution had no need to rely on the defendant's alleged complicity in the murder as part of their case on the charge of robbery; on the contrary, evidence of the murder was irrelevant to that charge.[25] This suggests that, where further proceedings are permitted by way of exception to the *Connelly* principle, on grounds of special circumstances, the rule in *Sambasivam* will in effect preclude such proceedings if (by contrast with *Connelly*) it is part of the prosecution's case on the second charge that the defendant was also guilty on the first. The flexibility of the *Connelly* principle seems to be undermined by the rigidity of the rule in *Sambasivam*.

8.18 We have provisionally proposed that the rule against double jeopardy should extend to cases in which the *Connelly* discretion exists, as well as those where the defendant is charged for a second time with the same offence. As in those cases which at present are covered by the autrefois rule, the rule in *Sambasivam* would be redundant in so far as it applied to prosecutions which were prohibited altogether by the new rule against double jeopardy; and, although it could not be allowed to apply in prosecutions brought by virtue of an exception to that rule, it

---

[20] See paras 2.15 – 2.18 and Part VI above.

[21] See Part V above.

[22] See para 2.21 above.

[23] [1998] QB 356.

[24] He pleaded guilty to a charge under the Health and Safety at Work Act 1974, and was later charged with manslaughter.

[25] [1964] AC 1254, 1342.

logically could not apply, because the acquittal would already have been quashed. In so far as the rule in *Sambasivam* is justified by the need to avoid double jeopardy, therefore, we believe that that need will be adequately served by our proposed rule against double jeopardy. If the rule in *Sambasivam* is to be retained, it will have to be justified on some other basis which applies to cases which do not involve double jeopardy.

CASES NOT INVOLVING DOUBLE JEOPARDY

8.19 The rule in *Sambasivam* applies equally where the defendant is charged with an offence other than the one of which he or she was previously acquitted, and even if the charges relate to different facts. In other words it can apply where the second prosecution does not amount to double jeopardy, and would not be prohibited by our proposed rule against double jeopardy. For example, where a person is acquitted on one charge and subsequently charged with committing a similar offence on another occasion, the prosecution may seek to adduce the evidence of the first alleged offence on the basis that it supports the evidence on the second. There is no element of double jeopardy here, because there is no question of the defendant now being *convicted* of the first offence. The evidence of the first offence is adduced solely for its relevance to the second. It will of course be prejudicial, and will therefore be inadmissible unless its prejudicial effect is outweighed by its probative value; but the rule in *Sambasivam* appears to make it inadmissible in any event, however great its probative value and however small its likely prejudicial effect.

8.20 In view of this overlap with the rules on the admissibility of a defendant's previous misconduct, we referred to the rule in our consultation paper on that subject.[26] We there provisionally proposed that evidence of previous misconduct which resulted in an acquittal should continue to be inadmissible.[27] Of those respondents who expressed a view on this proposal, the majority agreed without comment.

8.21 Jenny McEwan and Michael Hirst disagreed, and argued that, if evidence of such conduct would otherwise be admissible, it should not be rendered inadmissible merely because the defendant has previously been acquitted in respect of it.[28] Both of them pointed out that it would be absurd to exclude evidence which is so probative that it would otherwise qualify for admission as similar fact evidence; and both gave variations on the facts of *Smith*[29] (the notorious "brides in the bath" case) as hypothetical examples. Professor McEwan wrote:

---

[26] Evidence in Criminal Proceedings: Previous Misconduct of a Defendant (1996) Consultation Paper No 141. We will make recommendations on this subject in a forthcoming report.

[27] Para 14.24.

[28] Professor McEwan doubted whether such evidence is inadmissible at present, and argued that, if it is, it ought not to be: "Law Commission Dodges the Nettles in Consultation Paper No 141" [1997] Crim LR 93, 94. Mr Hirst thought it "not entirely clear" whether such evidence is inadmissible, but agreed with us that the weight of authority pointed in that direction.

[29] (1916) 11 Cr App R 229. Smith was charged with the murder of his common law wife Bessie Munday, who had been found dead in her bath. At trial, evidence was adduced regarding the

If in *Smith*[30] the defendant had been accused of the murder of his second wife, who was found dead in her bath, he might well have been acquitted for want of convincing evidence. But when his third wife was discovered dead in her bath, bringing the total of "Brides in the Bath" to three, it would be absurd if the prosecution could not adduce evidence of *both* former incidents, in order to prove the murder of the third wife, notwithstanding a previous acquittal in relation to one of them.

8.22 Michael Hirst has posed an even more telling example.

Imagine that D has been charged with a murder, and acquitted in controversial circumstances; imagine then that some months later a similar offence is committed, and that it is clear for various reasons that whoever committed the first offence also committed the second. Moreover, D seems to be the only person who could have been involved in both incidents. The *Sambasivam* rule would preclude use of that crucial similar fact evidence.[31]

8.23 He also pointed to the decision in *Humphrys*,[32] where the House of Lords held that, on a charge of committing perjury in a previous trial which ended in the defendant's acquittal, the prosecution could adduce evidence inconsistent with that acquittal. Mr Hirst argued that *Humphrys* "is not really distinguishable (though it purports to be) and yet reaches a totally different conclusion". We are inclined to agree that *Humphrys* cannot be reconciled with *Sambasivam* on any sensible basis, and that the conflict between them should be resolved; but it could be resolved in either direction. Mr Hirst argues that *Humphrys* should prevail. Peter Mirfield prefers *Sambasivam*, and indeed has argued that the criminal courts should recognise a doctrine of issue estoppel.[33]

Justifications for the rule

8.24 The effect of the rule in *Sambasivam*, in cases not involving double jeopardy, is to exclude relevant evidence on the ground that the issues to which the evidence is relevant have already been conclusively determined in favour of the defence. As Professor Sir John Smith has pointed out, "Estoppel, like other exclusionary rules, is an obstacle to the discovery of truth and therefore needs justification on grounds of policy".[34] We believe that the onus of justifying the rule is on those who would preserve it or extend it.

---

deaths of two other women who had lived with Smith, who had both died in their baths in a very similar way to Bessie Munday.

[30] (1916) 11 Cr App R 229. (Footnote supplied)

[31] "Contradicting Previous Acquittals" [1991] Crim LR 510, 517.

[32] [1977] AC 1.

[33] "Shedding a Tear for Issue Estoppel" [1980] Crim LR 336.

[34] [1974] Crim LR 248, 249. This observation was quoted with approval by Lord Edmund-Davies in *Humphrys* [1977] AC 1, at p 52.

8.25   Peter Mirfield bases his argument for the recognition of issue estoppel in criminal law on two policies: that of avoiding double jeopardy and that of finality. We have explained that the rule in *Sambasivam* is not required for the former purpose.[35] Mr Mirfield expresses the latter as follows:

> It is one of the most obvious and necessary purposes of any litigation before a court to establish (subject to appeals) the position as between the litigants for all time. Litigation should settle disputes finally and not simply decide them temporarily until some other decision be taken. Furthermore, if the unappealed or unsuccessfully appealed decision of one court may be re-opened by another court, there is a clear danger of the two courts reaching inconsistent decisions. An inconsistency between two judicial decisions in relation to the same question is likely to bring the law into disrepute. … It does not seem reasonable to argue that this policy is less relevant in criminal proceedings than in civil proceedings.[36]

8.26   Similarly, Martin Friedland argues that

> As a matter of fundamental policy in the administration of the criminal law it must be accepted by the Crown in a subsequent criminal proceeding that an acquittal is the equivalent to a finding of innocence.[37]

8.27   In support of this proposition Friedland cites *Plummer*,[38] where the appellant and two others were charged with conspiracy to defraud. The appellant pleaded guilty; the other two pleaded not guilty and were acquitted. Clearly the appellant could not be guilty of conspiring with the others if they were not guilty of conspiring with him. This led to discussion of the nature of a finding of not guilty. Bruce J referred to a note in *Russell on Crimes*[39] where it was suggested that a verdict of not guilty was not to be taken as establishing the innocence of the person acquitted, since the verdict may merely reflect a lack of evidence of guilt. Bruce J said: "It is a very dangerous principle to adopt to regard a verdict of not guilty as not fully establishing the innocence of the person to whom it relates."[40] Friedland continues:

---

[35]   See para 8.18 above.

[36]   [1980] Crim LR 336, 336–337.

[37]   *Double Jeopardy* (1969) p 129.

[38]   [1902] 2 KB 339, 349; overruled in *DPP v Shannon* [1975] AC 717.

[39]   4th ed, vol iii, p 146.

[40]   Cf *Villemaire v The Queen* (1962) 39 CR 297, 300, in which the majority held that an acquittal of the accused when the only issue raised was identity "only means that the jury was of the opinion that the appellant had not been identified as the person who had broken into the room: it cannot be read as a finding that the offence had been committed or attempted by some person other than the accused".

In most cases it would not be known whether the jury's verdict was because of a reasonable doubt or a finding of innocence. Fairness to the accused demands that it be assumed to be the latter.[41]

8.28 We have already considered the need for finality, in relation to possible exceptions to the rule against double jeopardy.[42] We there pointed out that there is no finality in the case of a conviction, and suggested that in criminal proceedings the advantages of finality may well be outweighed by other considerations. We agree, of course, that an acquitted defendant, like anyone else, should be entitled to the benefit of the presumption of innocence. But that presumption is rebuttable by proof of guilt. The question is whether, in the case of an acquitted defendant, it should become irrebuttable, in whatever criminal proceedings the question may arise. As Lord Devlin put it, in the context of whether the criminal law should recognise the doctrine of issue estoppel:

> The defence rightly enjoys the privilege of not having to prove anything; it has only to raise a reasonable doubt. Is it also to have the right to say that a fact which it has raised a reasonable doubt about is to be treated as conclusively established in its favour?[43]

8.29 The danger of two courts literally "reaching inconsistent decisions" would not arise unless the second prosecution is based on the same facts as the first; and that would be a case of double jeopardy, which we propose to control without resort to the rule in *Sambasivam*. We are here concerned not with double jeopardy, but with reliance on the defendant's alleged guilt on one occasion as probative of his or her guilt on another, when the defendant has already been acquitted in relation to the first. The only possible inconsistency is that the fact-finders in the second trial might regard the first offence as proved, and treat the defendant's guilt of that offence as probative of the offence charged, whereas the fact-finders in the first trial did not find it proved. Admittedly it might be clear that the prosecution in the second trial would have no case if it were not for the evidence of the first offence, so that a conviction of the second offence would necessarily imply a finding of guilt on the first. But this would simply mean that the fact-finders did not regard the case as proved beyond reasonable doubt, whereas the fact-finders in the second case did. The possibility of disagreement between different fact-finders, even on the same evidence, is unavoidable, particularly in a system which relies primarily on lay fact-finders. It is hard to see why the revelation of disagreement in a particular case should "bring the law into disrepute".

8.30 It should be repeated that, although the allegation which *Sambasivam* prevents the prosecution from making is normally[44] an allegation of criminal misconduct, the rule is not needed in order to protect the defendant from evidence which is unfairly prejudicial. If the rule did not exist, the defendant would still be protected

---

[41] *Double Jeopardy* (1969) p 129.

[42] See para 4.8 above.

[43] *Connelly v DPP* [1964] AC 1254, 1346.

[44] Because normally the prosecution will be precluded only from asserting the defendant's guilt of the former charge, not from repeating individual allegations that formed part of their case in relation to that charge: see para 8.12 above.

by the ordinary rules on the admissibility of prejudicial evidence. It would not be possible to adduce evidence of another offence allegedly committed by the defendant unless the probative value of that evidence outweighed its likely prejudicial effect. The question is whether, where the defendant has been *acquitted* of that offence, the evidence should still be inadmissible even if its probative value *does* outweigh its prejudicial effect.

The limitations of issue estoppel

8.31 Our provisional view is that, in its application to cases not involving double jeopardy, the rule in *Sambasivam* is in effect a kind of attenuated counterpart of the civil law doctrine of issue estoppel. If it is to be justified on that basis, it is arguable that it should be subject to the same limitations as that doctrine.[45] There are at least three such limitations which may be significant. First, the doctrine does not apply to a decision procured by fraud. Second, it appears not to apply where new evidence has become available. And third, it relates to the *issues* between the parties, not the evidence adduced.

Acquittals secured by fraud

8.32 The doctrine of issue estoppel does not apply to a decision procured by fraud, such as perjured evidence.[46] The decision in *Humphrys* might have been reached on this more limited ground, rather than on the ground that the doctrine has no application in criminal law at all.

> If a decision which would otherwise be res judicata can be impugned if the court has been deceived by false evidence, as it clearly can, it would indeed be remarkable if that decision operated as a bar to a prosecution for perjury in giving that false evidence.

> If this is the position in civil cases, it must also be the same in criminal for if the doctrine of issue estoppel is imported into the criminal law, surely this part of the doctrine must also be imported.[47]

---

[45] In *Humphrys* [1977] AC 1 at p 30, Lord Hailsham said:

> I agree with Diplock LJ in *Mills v Cooper* [1967] 2 QB 459, 469 where, in effect, he says that, if the doctrine of issue estoppel is applicable at all to criminal proceedings, it must be taken for better or for worse, with all its incidents. In other words, there cannot be a case where a party is entitled in criminal proceedings to pray in aid the doctrine of issue estoppel as it has come to be understood where he would not be entitled to do so in civil proceedings which is the forum in which the doctrine has been developed.

> Peter Mirfield, in arguing for the doctrine to be extended to criminal law, concedes that the same limitations would have to apply.

[46] *Duchess of Kingston's Case* (1776) 2 Smith LC 644, 651; *Abouloff v Oppenheimer & Co* (1882) 10 QBD 295; *Vadala v Lawes* (1890) 25 QBD 310; *Birch v Birch* [1902] P 62, [1902] P 130 (CA).

[47] *Humphrys* [1977] AC 1, 21, *per* Viscount Dilhorne.

New evidence

8.33 More generally, there is authority for the proposition that the civil law doctrine has no application where new evidence has become available since the issue was determined. In *Mills v Cooper*[48] Diplock LJ stated the doctrine as follows:

> [A] party to civil proceedings is not entitled to make, as against the other party, an assertion, whether of fact or of the legal consequences of facts, the correctness of which is an essential element in his cause of action or defence, if the same assertion was an essential element in his previous cause of action or defence in previous civil proceedings between the same parties or their predecessors in title and was found by a court of competent jurisdiction in such previous civil proceedings to be incorrect, *unless further material which is relevant to the correctness or incorrectness of the assertion and could not by reasonable diligence have been adduced by that party in the previous proceedings has since become available to him.*[49]

This passage was quoted without disapproval in *Humphrys*, and Lord Hailsham drew attention to the words in italics.[50] Peter Mirfield, while arguing that the doctrine should be extended to criminal law, points out that this qualification would presumably apply.[51]

8.34 The arguments for making the rule in *Sambasivam* subject to an exception for new evidence are similar to those for creating such an exception to the rule against double jeopardy. But, since the effect of the rule in *Sambasivam* is to prevent the prosecution not just from again seeking a conviction of the first offence but even from adducing evidence of it in proceedings for another offence, the arguments for an exception are even stronger than in the case of the rule against double jeopardy. It would be absurd if the discovery of new evidence enabled the prosecution to charge the defendant with the same offence for a second time, but not to assert the defendant's guilt of that offence in proceedings for another offence. Since we have provisionally proposed that there should be an exception to the latter rule in the case of new evidence, it follows that in our view the rule in *Sambasivam* should at least be made subject to such an exception, if it is retained at all. This would avoid the most absurd consequences of the rule.[52]

Issues and evidence

8.35 Issue estoppel relates to *issues*, not to the evidence that may be adduced in relation to them. In civil law the issues between the parties can be distilled from the pleadings, by ascertaining which of the allegations formally made by one side are

---

[48] [1967] 2 QB 459, 468–469. This was a criminal case. On the facts, the Divisional Court held that the doctrine would not apply anyway, even if it applied in criminal law at all, which was doubted.

[49] Italics supplied.

[50] [1977] AC 1, 39.

[51] [1980] Crim LR 336, 341–342.

[52] See paras 8.21 – 8.22 above.

denied (or not admitted) by the other; and only those issues become res judicatae when the case is determined. In *Mills v Cooper*[53] Diplock LJ said:

> Whatever may be said of other rules of law to which the label of "estoppel" is attached, "issue estoppel" is not a rule of evidence. True, ... it has the effect of preventing the party "estopped" from calling evidence to show that the assertion which is the subject of the "issue estoppel" is incorrect, but that is because the existence of the "issue estoppel" results in there being no issue in the subsequent civil proceedings to which such evidence would be relevant.

And in his formulation of the rule he referred to an assertion "the correctness of which is *an essential element* in [a party's] cause of action or defence, if the same assertion was *an essential element* in his previous cause of action or defence."[54]

8.36 By analogy, one would expect a criminal law version of the doctrine to rule out only those proceedings where an essential element of the offence charged (more familiarly known as a fact in issue) has been negated by the verdict in a previous trial. For example, if D is acquitted of assaulting V, issue estoppel would protect D from subsequently being charged with assault occasioning actual bodily harm in relation to the same incident, because the first trial would have determined that D did not commit the assault which is an essential element of assault occasioning actual bodily harm. But if D were charged with assaulting V on some later occasion, and evidence of the previous alleged assault were thought sufficiently probative to justify its admission (for example as throwing light on the relationship between D and V),[55] issue estoppel would not arise: D's guilt of the previous assault would not be an *element* of the offence charged, but only *evidence* of one or more such elements. Yet it seems that the rule in *Sambasivam* would render such evidence inadmissible. In *G v Coltart*,[56] for instance, the theft of which the defendant had been acquitted was evidence of, not an element of, the theft charged; but it was held inadmissible.

8.37 The analogy with issue estoppel therefore suggests that the rule in *Sambasivam*, if it is to be retained at all, should apply only where the defendant's guilt of the first offence is not just *evidence* of the offence now charged but an essential element of it, a "fact in issue". But that would mean confining the rule to the situation where both charges arise out of the same facts – that is, double jeopardy. We have already pointed out that there is no need to retain the rule for the purpose of avoiding double jeopardy. It must have some application to cases *not* involving double jeopardy to be worth retaining at all. And the analogy with issue estoppel suggests that it should have no application to any such cases.

---

[53] [1967] 2 QB 459, 469.

[54] Italics supplied.

[55] Cf *Fulcher* [1995] 2 Cr App R 251.

[56] [1967] 1 QB 432. See para 8.3 above.

Conclusion

8.38 In this part we have argued that the rule in *Sambasivam* has two distinct applications. First, it protects the defendant against double jeopardy, by preventing the prosecution from bringing another charge inconsistent with a previous acquittal. But, given our proposal that the rule against double jeopardy should be retained and indeed extended, the rule in *Sambasivam* is not needed for this purpose. In this respect it is harmless, provided it is subject to the same exceptions as the double jeopardy rule, but redundant.

8.39 The second application of the rule is in the case where the charge laid is not itself inconsistent with the previous acquittal, but the prosecution seeks to adduce evidence which, if accepted, means that the defendant must have been guilty of the offence of which he or she was acquitted. In this context the rule seems to work as a kind of issue estoppel. But even in civil law the doctrine of issue estoppel is subject to certain qualifications, which must be equally applicable to any counterpart of that doctrine in criminal law. For example, it apparently does not apply where new evidence has emerged since the previous decision. Moreover, it does not render evidence inadmissible: it states that, once an issue has been determined, it is *no longer an issue* in subsequent proceedings between the same parties. In criminal law this would presumably mean only that the defendant cannot be charged with an offence if one of the *elements* of that offence (not just the evidence of it) is the defendant's guilt of an offence of which he or she has already been acquitted. But in that case the charge would arise out of the same facts as the first. It would therefore be a case of double jeopardy. It seems to follow that the rule in *Sambasivam* cannot properly be applied outside the context of double jeopardy – where it is redundant.

8.40 **We provisionally propose that**

(1) **subject to the rule against double jeopardy and the rules on the admissibility of evidence of a defendant's previous misconduct, the rule in *Sambasivam* (which prevents the prosecution from making an assertion which is inconsistent with a previous acquittal of the defendant) should be abolished; and**

(2) **if, contrary to our proposal, the rule is retained, it should not apply to an assertion supported by new evidence which could not with due diligence have been adduced at the first trial.**

PART IX
ACQUITTAL AND CONVICTION

9.1 The three doctrines discussed in this paper (the autrefois rule, the *Connelly*[1] principle and the rule in *Sambasivam*)[2] apply only where the defendant has previously been acquitted or (in the case of the first two) convicted of an offence. There is rarely any difficulty in determining whether this requirement is satisfied: the line currently drawn between an acquittal or conviction on the one hand, and some other conclusion to criminal proceedings on the other, is fairly clear. But it may be arguable that that line should be drawn in a different place.[3]

NARROWING THE CONCEPT OF AN ACQUITTAL OR CONVICTION

9.2 In this section we discuss some situations in which, at present, the defendant is regarded as having been acquitted (or, in one case,[4] convicted) for the purposes of the various rules concerned with double jeopardy, and it is arguable that, for the purposes of a reformed rule against double jeopardy, he or she should not be so regarded. The scope of the rule would thus be reduced.

Delaying the point in proceedings at which the rule applies

9.3 It is possible under the current law for the prosecution to abandon the proceedings without precluding subsequent proceedings for the same offence. Before committal, or the start of a *summary* trial, section 23 of the Prosecution of Offences Act 1985 gives the CPS power to discontinue the proceedings, and it is expressly provided that discontinuance "shall not prevent the institution of fresh proceedings in respect of the same offence".[5] Section 23A, inserted by the Crime and Disorder Act 1998,[6] will, when brought into force throughout England and Wales,[7] make similar provision for the discontinuance of proceedings for offences triable only on indictment, which under section 51 of the 1998 Act will be automatically sent to the Crown Court without the need for a committal. In these cases the power to discontinue will lapse when the indictment is preferred. These statutory powers are additional to the power (which prosecutors already had before 1985) to withdraw a charge in the magistrates' court.[8] But the prosecution cannot drop the case after committal without a verdict of not guilty being entered,

---

[1] [1964] AC 1254; see para 2.21 above.

[2] [1950] AC 458; see Part VIII above.

[3] Our freedom to draw the line elsewhere is to a degree circumscribed by the fact that the Strasbourg Court will not be bound in its own interpretation of the terms "conviction" and "acquittal" in Article 4 by their meanings in our system. For the Court's approach to such terms, see para 3.35 above.

[4] Viz that of a conviction in another jurisdiction: see paras 9.10 – 9.15 below.

[5] Section 23(9).

[6] Section 119 and Sch 8, para 64.

[7] In certain areas it came into force on 4 January 1999: Crime and Disorder Act 1998 (Commencement No 2 and Transitional Provisions) Order 1998, SI 1998 No 2327.

[8] *R v DPP, ex p Cooke* (1992) 95 Cr App R 233.

thus triggering the autrefois rule.[9] Committal, or preferment of the indictment where there is no committal, is the point of no return.

9.4 It would be possible for the double jeopardy rule to come into play at some later point. Two possible rules suggest themselves. The first is that no acquittal should count for the purpose of the double jeopardy rule unless it is an acquittal by the jury after full consideration of the evidence. It would thus exclude acquittals directed by the judge (for instance, following a successful submission of no case to answer, or a decision by the prosecution as its case emerges that it cannot ask the jury to convict), as well as acquittals directed by the judge under section 17 of the Criminal Justice Act 1967. The second is that the prosecution should be entitled to withdraw a charge at any time up to the commencement of the trial, but no later.

9.5 We provisionally reject the first option. It would mean that a defendant could be tried again, possibly before a judge more sympathetic to the prosecution, even after all of the prosecution's evidence had been heard. It would provide an unfair disincentive to the making of submissions of no case to answer. Finally, it would be liable to a challenge under the ECHR, on the basis that a directed acquittal would probably count as an acquittal for the purposes of Article 4, even if were deemed *not* to count as one for the purposes of the domestic law of double jeopardy.

9.6 Given that one of the main functions of the double jeopardy rule is to protect a defendant from the stress and inconvenience of facing two trials rather than one, the second option could be attractive. The primary function of committal is to give the defence an opportunity to argue that there is no case. There is no obvious logic in treating it also as the cut-off point for the purposes of the rule against double jeopardy. In our view, however, a defendant is entitled to expect accurate assessment of his or her case, and sound decision-making by the prosecutor, at a reasonably early stage. Committal (or preferment, where there is no committal) is the earliest reasonable stage, given the realities of the criminal justice system. The prosecutor must have *some* opportunity to abandon the case without penalty, because the proceedings are usually initiated by the police before the prosecutor sees the file. But the decision whether to commit requires the prosecutor to make a positive decision about the case. It therefore seems reasonable that the protection afforded by the double jeopardy rule should begin at that point.

9.7 Indeed, it is difficult to see what would be a legitimate motive for the prosecution to withdraw a charge after committal. If it sees no prospect of ever being able to seek a conviction, we think it is right that a verdict of not guilty should be recorded. The prosecution might wish to leave the door open for further proceedings in the event of further evidence becoming available, but that possibility would be better catered for by our proposed exception to the double

---

[9] The prosecution may ask the Attorney-General to enter a nolle prosequi, which has the effect of staying the indictment and does not preclude subsequent proceedings for the same offence; but this is normally done only where the defendant is unfit to stand trial, not where the prosecution discovers weaknesses in its case.

jeopardy rule in the case of new evidence.[10] If the case is one in which the new evidence exception could not apply, because of the safeguards built into the proposal,[11] it would be equally wrong to allow the prosecution to drop the case in the hope that new evidence will emerge. On the other hand, if the prosecution cannot proceed because of a temporary problem, such as a witness being unavailable, the proper course would be to seek an adjournment. If the judge refused an adjournment, allowing the prosecution to withdraw the indictment altogether, without a verdict being recorded, would amount to allowing the prosecution to overturn the decision of the judge.

9.8 Such a change in the law might also be vulnerable to a challenge under the ECHR. We cannot be sure that the Strasbourg Court would regard some forms of pre-trial termination as acquittals for the purposes of Article 4; but the fact that the law had been *changed* so as to prevent such a termination from counting as an acquittal might well be of considerable significance. The Court has made it clear that it will not allow states to evade Convention rights merely by relabelling their procedures.[12] Moreover, any delay in the *final* determination of the case would be difficult to justify in terms of the Article 6 requirement of a hearing within a reasonable time, if it were occasioned by the late withdrawal of a charge.

9.9 We find these arguments persuasive. **Our provisional view is that, for the purposes of the rule against double jeopardy and (if, contrary to the proposal at paragraph 8.40 above, it is retained) the rule in *Sambasivam*, a person should continue to be regarded as having been acquitted**

    (1) where a jury return a verdict of not guilty, with or without consideration of the evidence; and

    (2) where the prosecution offers no evidence.

Acquittal or conviction in another jurisdiction

9.10 There is one situation in which a subsequent prosecution for the same offence seems to be prohibited by the autrefois rule but not by Article 4(1): namely where the defendant has been acquitted or convicted in another jurisdiction. It is generally believed that, in such a case, the autrefois rule would preclude a subsequent prosecution in England and Wales on the same facts.[13] But the

---

[10] See Part V above.

[11] For example, cases which are insufficiently serious to bring the exception into play. See para 5.27 above.

[12] See, eg, *Engel v The Netherlands (No 1)* A 22 (1976).

[13] *Aughet* (1919) 13 Cr App R 101, confirmed, obiter, in *Treacy v DPP* [1971] AC 537, *per* Lord Diplock who stated that the doctrine of autrefois acquit and convict "has always applied whether the previous conviction or acquittal ... was by an English court or by a foreign court" (at p 562D). There is an exception if the defendant was convicted in his or her absence and there is no likelihood of his or her returning to serve the sentence: *Thomas* [1985] QB 604. The assumption is not easy to reconcile with the decision in *Beedie* [1998] QB 356 that the autrefois rule applies only where the second prosecution is for an offence which is *in law* the same as the one of which the defendant has been acquitted or convicted.

Explanatory Report to Protocol 7[14] makes it clear that the words "under the jurisdiction of the same State" are intended to limit the operation of Article 4(1) to the national level.[15] Article 4(1) therefore does not prohibit successive prosecutions for the same offence in different countries, and the new rule against double jeopardy need not do so in order to ensure compliance.

9.11   Another international instrument, however, has the opposite effect. Article 54 of the Schengen Convention provides:

> Persons on whom final judgment has been passed in one Contracting Party may not be prosecuted by another Contracting Party for the same offences provided that, where they are sentenced, the sentence has been served or is currently being served or can no longer be enforced under the sentencing law of the Contracting Party delivering the sentence.

The UK and Ireland are the only European Union countries who are not signatories to the Schengen Convention, which is now part of the EU.[16]

9.12   The UK is, therefore, strictly unconstrained in deciding whether to apply the double jeopardy rule to foreign acquittals and convictions. There are arguments on both sides. On the one hand, it could be seen as anomalous that the defendant can escape punishment in England and Wales because he or she has been unsuccessfully prosecuted in another jurisdiction, if, in England and Wales, the first prosecution would not have come to trial (because there was insufficient evidence for the CPS to prosecute, and a private prosecution would have been taken over and discontinued) or might have resulted in a conviction (because of some rule that makes convictions harder to obtain in the other jurisdiction).

---

[14]   CE Doc H (83) 3.

[15]   Para 27. The report mentions three other European Council conventions. The European Convention on Extradition (European Convention on Extradition Order 1990 (SI 1990 No 1507), Sch 1, Article 9) requires that those upon whom final judgment has been passed by the state requested to extradite, in respect of the offence for which extradition is sought, shall not be extradited; and it allows the requested state to refuse to extradite those against whom it has decided not to institute, or has terminated, proceedings in respect of the same offence. The UK has not ratified the European Convention on the International Validity of Criminal Judgments, which allows one state to request another to enforce a sentence under certain conditions (Articles 53–55 relate to *ne bis in idem*); nor the European Convention on the Transfer of Proceedings in Criminal Matters, which provides a mechanism for states to request other states to prosecute a person resident in, or a national of, the requested state for an offence under the law of the requesting state (Articles 35–37 relate to *ne bis in idem*).

[16]   The collection of instruments known as the Schengen *acquis*, of which the Convention forms a part, arose out of an initiative which was independent of the EU. As a result of the Amsterdam Treaty, however, it has now been incorporated into the Union. The UK and Ireland have exercised an opt-out which is provided for in the Treaty. The purpose of the Schengen process was the abolition of internal border controls in favour of control at the common external frontier. It also includes elements such as police co-operation, information systems, data protection and information on asylum matters. A brief account of the main features is given in Part 2 of the 31st Report of the House of Lords Select Committee on European Communities (HL 62).

9.13 On the other hand, if it is wrong to bring a second prosecution when both trials are in England and Wales, the same considerations must in general make it equally wrong to prosecute a person who has already been tried elsewhere. Further, failure to apply the double jeopardy rule to acquittals and convictions in another country would imply a critical stance towards that country's criminal justice system, which would sit uneasily with our obligations to extradite people accused by the majority of foreign jurisdictions.[17] It would also seem anomalous in the case of countries which are bound by the ECHR.

9.14 On balance, we consider that the arguments in favour of continuing to recognise foreign acquittals and convictions are stronger than those against. Moreover, it is likely that at some time in the future the UK may wish to adopt the Schengen *acquis*. That decision would be a political and diplomatic one, the merits of which are not within our competence. It would be undesirable for the law to be changed in advance of that decision in such a way as to inhibit the Government's freedom of action.[18] While Schengen itself applies only to members of the European Union, we provisionally consider that it would be wrong in principle for *some* foreign verdicts to count for the purpose of the double jeopardy rule, but not others.

9.15 **We invite views on whether the rule against double jeopardy and (if, contrary to the proposal at paragraph 8.40 above, it is retained) the rule in *Sambasivam* should apply**

> (1) **wherever the previous acquittal or conviction occurred;**
>
> (2) **unless the previous acquittal or conviction was in one of certain countries expressly excluded for this purpose;[19]**
>
> (3) **only if the previous acquittal or conviction was in a member state of the European Union; or**
>
> (4) **only if the previous acquittal or conviction was in England and Wales.[20]**

We provisionally favour the first option.

EXTENDING THE CONCEPT OF AN ACQUITTAL OR CONVICTION

9.16 As we have explained,[21] there are a number of ways in which criminal proceedings can come to an end without the defendant being acquitted or convicted. In these

---

[17] Written Answer, *Hansard* (HC) 5 July 1999, vol 334, col 326.

[18] There might in fact be two decisions for the Government to make. If it were decided to join the Schengen *acquis* as a whole, the Government would still have the option of taking advantage of a specific provision to derogate from Article 54. The argument that the Government should have freedom of manoeuvre applies equally to both decisions.

[19] We would be grateful if anyone supporting this option could indicate how such an exceptional country could be identified.

[20] We would be grateful if anyone supporting this option could indicate how acquittals and convictions in Scotland and Northern Ireland should be treated.

[21] See para 3.34 above.

circumstances the various rules protecting the defendant against double jeopardy do not apply. It would be possible to amend the law so that, in some of these circumstances, the defendant *is* regarded as having been acquitted or convicted; and in that case the new rule against double jeopardy *would* apply.

Outcomes which arguably should count as an acquittal

9.17 In the case of some of these outcomes, such a change would make no sense, because preserving the possibility of further proceedings is, at least in part, the object of the exercise. This is true, for example, of an order that a count lie on the file, not to be proceeded with without the consent of the court or the Court of Appeal. Such an order is commonly made where the defendant pleads guilty on some counts and the prosecution does not seek convictions on the rest, but an acquittal is thought to be inappropriate.

9.18 Similar considerations apply, in our view, to the discharge of a jury without their reaching a verdict. If this were regarded as having the same effect as an acquittal, the effect would be to tilt the balance dramatically in favour of the defendant: instead of requiring a majority of ten to two, an acquittal would require only three jurors to be in favour (that is, enough to rule out the ten-two majority required for a conviction).

9.19 It may be arguable that the prosecution should not be able to withdraw a charge in the magistrates' court, or to serve a notice of discontinuance, while retaining the right to renew the charge at a later date. But the power to discontinue is a crucial feature of the system set up by the Prosecution of Offences Act 1985. It is a corollary of the fact that in most cases proceedings will already have been initiated before the CPS has a chance to decide whether its criteria for prosecution are satisfied. To abolish this power (or to equate it with the offering of no evidence, which does count as an acquittal) would hamper the administration of justice for no great benefit. It should be remembered that the resurrection of a discontinued charge, without good reason for the change of mind, might be treated as an abuse of process, and might also infringe the defendant's right to be treated fairly under Article 6 of the ECHR.

Outcomes which arguably should count as a conviction

9.20 In *Richards*[22] the Privy Council held that, for the purpose of the plea of autrefois convict, there is no conviction until sentence is passed. Earlier authorities to the contrary were disapproved.[23] If, as we have argued, the main function of the autrefois rule is to protect the defendant from the distress of a second trial after the first has proceeded to a verdict, it may be arguable that that protection should

---

[22] [1993] AC 217.

[23] *Sheridan* [1937] 1 KB 223; *Grant* [1936] 2 All ER 1156. In each of these cases it was held that the defendant could not be tried on indictment after being convicted by (or pleading guilty before) magistrates, where, upon hearing of his previous convictions, the magistrates decided to commit him or her for trial. This situation could not arise now that a magistrates' court has power to commit the defendant to the Crown Court for sentence only: Magistrates' Courts Act 1980, s 38.

be conferred as soon as a valid verdict is returned. But, as the Privy Council pointed out, it would be absurd if a defendant could not be rearraigned where the judge died between verdict and sentence.[24] Our provisional view is that where, after a verdict of guilty, some such unexpected event prevents sentence from being passed, the situation is analogous to that of the jury failing to agree, and that the rule against double jeopardy should not apply.

9.21 It is arguable that taking an offence into consideration on sentence should preclude subsequent proceedings, on the ground that it is tantamount to a conviction and sentence for that offence. There is authority that this course does preclude subsequent proceedings,[25] but that authority has been doubted[26] and the autrefois rule is generally believed not to apply. It is only in exceptional circumstances that the question would be likely to arise.

Conclusion

9.22 It seems to us that in all these cases the defendant is sufficiently protected from oppressive prosecuting by the jurisdiction to stay proceedings which are an abuse of process, a jurisdiction which is bolstered by (and must now be exercised with a view to) the defendant's right to a fair trial under Article 6. In the light of these safeguards, we do not think there is any injustice in allowing these cases to remain outside the rule against double jeopardy. However, **we invite views on whether, for the purposes of the rule against double jeopardy and (if, contrary to the proposal at paragraph 8.40, it is retained) the rule in *Sambasivam*, any outcome of criminal proceedings which does not now count as an acquittal or conviction should count as such.**

---

[24] [1993] AC 217, 226G.

[25] *McMinn* (1945) 30 Cr App R 138.

[26] *Nicholson* [1947] 2 All ER 535.

PART X
RETROSPECTIVE EFFECT

10.1 In this part we consider whether our proposals should be retrospective, in the sense of being applied in relation to acquittals and convictions which have taken place before our proposals come into force. Both the ECHR and domestic law in principle oppose retrospective criminal legislation. There is, however, an exception (clear in the case of the ECHR, more doubtfully in English law) for *procedural* legislation. We make no proposal on this issue; but we invite views as to whether, even if it is feasible to give our proposals retrospective effect, it would be right to do so.

THE PRINCIPLE

10.2 Retrospective criminal legislation is generally held to be inherently unfair and contrary to principle. As Willes J said in 1870:

> Retrospective laws are ... contrary to the general principle that legislation by which the conduct of mankind is to be regulated ought, when introduced for the first time, to deal with future acts, and ought not to change the character of past transactions carried on upon the faith of the then existing law.[1]

10.3 The principle can be derived from the fundamental constitutional doctrine of the rule of law.[2] The state should only punish a person for breaking the law. A person is entitled to do, and should not be punished for doing, that which is not forbidden. It follows that the state should not *later* forbid, and punish, that which was not forbidden at the time.

10.4 In pre-Convention English law, this principle is reflected in a presumption of statutory interpretation. As stated by Francis Bennion, the rule is that "Unless the contrary intention appears, an enactment is presumed not to be intended to have a retrospective operation."[3]

10.5 The principle appears in more substantive form (although confined to criminal matters) in Article 7 of the ECHR.[4] The article provides:

> No one shall be held guilty of any criminal offence on account of any act or omission which did not constitute a criminal offence under

---

[1] *Phillips v Eyre* (1870) 6 QB 1, 23. The case approved a retrospective colonial indemnity act which removed the right to sue for torts committed by the Governor during the suppression of a rebellion in Jamaica. See also, eg, *Re Athlumney* [1898] 2 QB 547, 552.

[2] Or the separation of powers: Charles Hochman, "The Supreme Court and the Constitutionality of Retroactive Legislation" 73 Harv LR 692 (1960), quoting Smead "The Rule Against Retroactive Legislation as a Principle of Jurisprudence" 20 Minn LR 775 (1936).

[3] *Statutory Interpretation* (3rd ed 1997) p 235.

[4] Article 7 also encapsulates a general principle of European Community law as declared by the European Court of Justice: *R v Kirk (Case 63/83)* [1985] 1 All ER 453, 462c.

national or international law at the time when it was committed. Nor shall a heavier penalty be imposed than the one that was applicable at the time the criminal offence was committed.

10.6 The first sentence of Article 7 prohibits the creation of retrospective offences by legislation, or through the development of the common law, so as to encompass conduct which would not previously have been regarded as a crime.[5] It also "embodies, more generally, the principle that only the law can define a crime ... and the principle that the criminal law must not be extensively construed to an accused's detriment".[6] The objective of this guarantee is to ensure that a person should be able to judge, at the time of engaging in particular conduct, whether or not it amounts to a crime.[7]

PROCEDURAL CHANGE

10.7 However, both in the ECHR and, at least arguably, in English law, the principle applies only to substantive law, not to merely procedural changes.

The ECHR

10.8 Article 7 does not prohibit retrospective changes in the rules of criminal procedure so as to remove a bar or obstacle to a prosecution.[8] The requirements of Article 7 are, in our view, satisfied if the conduct in question constituted a crime at the time when the offence was committed: it is immaterial that the procedural rules in existence at the time of an acquittal or conviction prevented it from being reopened. Article 7 would not prevent the reopening of such an acquittal or conviction under provisions subsequently coming into force.

English law

10.9 It appears that the same distinction has been accepted in English criminal law: "The general rule against the retrospective operation of statutes does not apply to procedural provisions".[9] Thus it would appear that on the face of it the proposals in this paper could properly be introduced with retrospective effect.[10]

---

5 *X Ltd and Y v UK* (1982) 28 DR 77.

6 *Kokkinakis v Greece* A 260-A (1993) at para 52.

7 *S W v UK* A 335-B (1995); *C R v UK* A 335-C (1995).

8 In *X v UK* (1976) 3 DR 95, for example, the Commission held that there was no violation of Article 7 where the Court of Appeal upheld the applicant's conviction by reference to an important precedent in the law of evidence which had been decided by the House of Lords after the conviction.

9 *Makanjuola and E* [1995] 2 Cr App R 469, 472, *per* Taylor CJ. See also *Chandra Dharma* [1905] 2 KB 335 (the extension of a limitation period for charging a sexual offence was purely procedural because it did not "alter the character of the offence, or take away any defence"). For a use of the distinction, see Eva Steiner "Prosecuting War Criminals in England and France" [1991] Crim LR 180.

10 Drawing the distinction between the substantive and the procedural is not always easy. For instance, in *Blyth v Blyth and Pugh* [1965] P 411, a divorce case, a change in the law allowing the admission of evidence to rebut what had previously been an irrebuttable presumption of condonation by sexual intercourse after knowledge of adultery was described as "purely

10.10　However, if the *argument* for the distinction between procedural and substantive retrospective effect is examined, the point becomes less clear. In *L'Office Cherifien des Phosphates v Yamashita-Shinnihon Steamship Co Ltd*,[11] Sir Thomas Bingham MR gave two possible reasons for the distinction. The first was that given in the following passage from Bennion:

> [A] procedural change is expected to improve matters for everyone concerned (or at least to improve matters for some, without inflicting detriment on anyone else who uses ordinary care, vigilance and promptness).[12]

The second was that

> No suitor has any vested interest in the course of procedure, nor any right to complain, if during the litigation the procedure is changed, provided, of course, that no injustice is done.[13]

10.11　So, although the conclusion has been applied in criminal cases, the reasoning behind it appears to be drawn from civil proceedings, and does not easily translate into a criminal context. Further, the exception to the general rule for procedural changes "only applies where application of it would not cause unfairness or injustice".[14] If this approach to procedural retrospectivity in civil proceedings is also applicable in the criminal context, the question of whether the existing state of English law presumes no retrospective effect is the same as the question whether retrospective effect is desirable (that is, fair and just).

THE DESIRABILITY OF RETROSPECTIVE EFFECT

10.12　Even if it were clear that the presumption against retrospectivity would not apply to our proposals, it would be wrong simply to assume that they should be introduced with retrospective effect for that reason alone.[15] The separate question is whether it is *desirable* that they should have retrospective effect.

---

procedural" because it related to the admission of evidence. On the other hand, in *Cruttenden* [1991] 2 QB 66 the Court of Appeal doubted that the change which allowed a wife to give evidence against her husband was purely procedural.

[11] [1994] 1 AC 486, 495.

[12] *Statutory Interpretation* (3rd ed 1997) p 239.

[13] *Republic of Costa Rica v Erlanger* (1876) 3 Ch D 62, 69 *per* Mellish LJ.

[14] *L'Office Cherifien des Phosphates v Yamashita-Shinnihon Steamship Co Ltd* [1994] 1 AC 486, 495, *per* Sir Thomas Bingham MR. The House of Lords in the same case also proceeded on the basis that the fundamental value was fairness: see particularly the speech of Lord Mustill, [1994] 1 AC 486, 524-525.

[15] It can be argued that there is an autonomous constitutional principle or convention, which "governs" what Parliament may properly legislate, and which is therefore antecedent to the presumption applied in the courts: see for instance Sheena McMurtrie "The Constitutionality of the War Crimes Act 1991" [1992] Stat LR 128. Our view is that, even if one assumes that there is such a principle, it must be coterminous with the presumption. If it were not, then the existence of the presumption would mean that the courts presume that Parliament will not (applying the "autonomous principle") legislate some unconstitutional retrospective measures, but do not presume likewise in respect of others.

10.13   On the one hand, whether or not the distinction between substantive and procedural legislative change is well founded in English law, there *is* clearly a significant difference in the degree of detriment involved. Legislation which is *substantively* retrospective renders criminal that which was not criminal when it was done. In the case of *procedurally* retrospective legislation, the act was criminal when it was done. The new procedures merely make it possible, or easier, to bring the offender to justice. It is clearly in the interests of criminals not to be prosecuted for their crimes; it is not in itself *unfair* for a procedural block to their prosecution to be removed.

10.14   On the other hand, one of the matters to be taken into account in determining whether it is in the interests of justice for the acquittal to be reopened, or whether the proposed retrial would be an abuse of process,[16] would be the possibility that the defendant has altered his or her position, to his or her detriment, in reliance on the belief that the acquittal could never be reopened. Such reliance would appear to be entirely reasonable in the present state of the law; and, if it were shown to have occurred, it may be hard to see how the defendant's position could be adequately protected against the unfairness that would result if that reliance turned out to be unfounded. It seems reasonable to assume that, for most people who have committed an offence of any seriousness, the possibility of being prosecuted (or re-prosecuted) for that offence is likely to exercise a substantial influence on the way in which they order their lives. Arguably, therefore, in the case of most defendants acquitted before our proposals came into force,[17] there would be an element of unfairness in quashing their acquittals. And in that case there might be little to be lost by simply exempting them from the new rules altogether.

10.15   Moreover, while provisionally proposing that it should in some circumstances be possible to reopen an acquittal on grounds of new evidence, we have also suggested that this possibility might be available only for a limited time after the acquittal. If this suggestion were adopted, it would automatically restrict the degree to which the exception *could* be retrospective. For example, if the time limit were one year, this would make it impossible to apply the new exception to any acquittal which had taken place more than one year before the exception came into force. It might be debatable whether the possibility of extending the exception to a handful of comparatively recent acquittals would justify the difficulties that retrospective effect would involve.

10.16   **We invite views as to whether, if our proposals were implemented, the legislation should apply to acquittals and convictions taking place before it comes into force.**

---

[16]   See Part VII above.

[17]   Or, perhaps, before it became clear that further exceptions to the autrefois rule might be introduced – eg the publication of a final recommendation of such a change by this Commission, or of this consultation paper, or of the Macpherson report. But in our view it would be unrealistic to allow such a factor to be crucial.

PART XI
PROSECUTION APPEALS

11.1 In Part III we suggested that the requirement of a *final* acquittal or conviction is best regarded, not as excluding certain acquittals and convictions from the ambit of Article 4, but as exempting certain *ways of challenging* a verdict (namely appeals) from the prohibition that Article 4 imposes. There is no breach of Article 4 in the fact that the prosecution already has certain rights of appeal in English law.[1] Nor would there be any necessary breach if those rights of appeal were extended.

11.2 It is clearly arguable that such an extension should be made, on grounds of consistency alone. At present, the prosecution has a right of appeal (albeit only on a point of law) against a summary acquittal, but not against an acquittal on indictment. A defendant who is convicted as a result of a misdirection can be retried once the conviction is quashed on appeal; a defendant wrongly acquitted on the judge's direction cannot. But it is also arguable that these apparent inconsistencies can be justified.

11.3 This is a large and difficult topic, and, in our view, severable from the central subject-matter of this paper. We therefore do not propose to examine the issues here. We realise of course that others may take a different view. **If any respondents believe that the law of double jeopardy cannot sensibly be reformed without also rationalising the law relating to prosecution appeals, we invite views on how this might be done.**

---

[1] See paras 2.11 – 2.13 above.

PART XII
PROVISIONAL PROPOSALS AND CONSULTATION ISSUES

In this part we list our provisional proposals and conclusions, and other issues on which we seek respondents' views. More generally, **we invite comments on *any* of the matters contained in, or issues raised by, this paper, and any other suggestions that respondents may wish to put forward. For the purpose of analysing the responses it would be very helpful if, as far as possible, they could refer to the numbering of the paragraphs in this part.**

THE RULE AGAINST DOUBLE JEOPARDY

1. We provisionally propose that

    (1)   the rule against double jeopardy should be retained;

    (2)   the rule should be extended so as to prohibit the prosecution of a person not only

        (a)   for any offence of which he or she has previously been acquitted or convicted, but also

        (b)   for any offence founded on the same or substantially the same facts as such an offence; and

    (3)   the rule as thus extended, and any exceptions to it, should be stated in statutory form.

                                                                            (paragraph 4.16)

NEW EVIDENCE

2. We provisionally propose that the rule against double jeopardy should be subject to an exception for certain cases where new evidence is discovered after an acquittal.

                                                                            (paragraph 5.17)

The seriousness of the offence

3. We provisionally propose that

    (1)   the exception for new evidence should be available only where, if the defendant were convicted of the offence now alleged, the sentence would be likely to be of a specified minimum severity; and

    (2)   for the purpose of determining what sentence would be likely to be imposed, it should be assumed

        (a)   that the plea would be one of not guilty;

(b)   that the court would find the facts to be as the prosecution now alleges them to be; and

(c)   that the sentence would not be reduced on the basis of any distress or uncertainty resulting from the retrial, or the lapse of time since the offence or the acquittal.

(paragraph 5.27)

4.   We invite views on what, for the purpose of the requirement proposed at paragraph 3 above, the specified minimum sentence should be. Our provisional preference is for a minimum of three years' imprisonment.

(paragraph 5.29)

The strength of the evidence

5.   We provisionally propose that the exception for new evidence should be available only where the new evidence makes the prosecution's case substantially stronger than it was at the first trial.

(paragraph 5.38)

6.   We provisionally propose that the exception for new evidence should be available only where, taking into account *all* the evidence likely to be adduced, the likelihood of the defendant being convicted at a retrial is judged by the court to be of a certain minimum level. The options for this minimum level include

(1)   that a reasonable jury, properly directed, would be more likely to convict than to acquit;

(2)   that it is highly probable that such a jury would convict; or

(3)   that the court is sure that such a jury would convict.

We provisionally reject (1), and invite views on (2) and (3).

(paragraph 5.42)

7.   We invite views on whether the minimum level of evidential strength required under the proposal in paragraph 6 above should be any lower where the previous prosecution was a private one.

(paragraph 5.45)

Evidence not available for the first trial

8.   We provisionally propose that

(1)   the power to reopen an acquittal on grounds of new evidence should be available only where that evidence could not, with due diligence, have been adduced at the first trial; but

(2) evidence which was not admissible in the first trial, and subsequently becomes admissible owing to a change in the law, should count as new evidence.

(paragraph 5.48)

The interests of justice

9. We provisionally propose that a retrial should be allowed on grounds of new evidence only where the court is satisfied that, in all the circumstances of the case, this is in the interests of justice.

(paragraph 5.51)

A time limit

10. We invite views as to whether an application to quash an acquittal on the grounds of new evidence should have to be made within a fixed period after the acquittal, and, if so, what that period should be.

(paragraph 5.57)

Successive retrials

11. We provisionally propose that

(1) the exception for new evidence should not be available where the acquittal was at a retrial which itself was held by virtue of that exception; but

(2) where the acquittal was at a retrial held on some other ground, this should be only one factor to be taken into account in determining whether another retrial would be in the interests of justice.

(paragraph 5.60)

The appropriate court

12. We provisionally propose

(1) that the decision whether to allow a retrial on grounds of new evidence should, in the first instance, be taken by the High Court;

(2) that there should be a right of appeal against a decision of the High Court to allow a retrial on those grounds; and

(3) that that right of appeal should be to the Criminal Division of the Court of Appeal.

We invite views as to whether the prosecution should have a right of appeal against a refusal to allow a retrial.

(paragraph 5.68)

New evidence relating to a different offence

13. We provisionally propose that, where the defendant has previously been tried for an offence, and new evidence suggests that he or she is guilty of a second, different, offence arising out of the same or substantially the same facts,

    (1) where the first trial resulted in a conviction, the High Court should have power to authorise a prosecution for the second offence;

    (2) the High Court should generally exercise its power (to authorise a prosecution for the second offence or to quash the acquital for the first) subject to the same conditions that, had the defendant been acquitted of the second offence at the time when he or she was convicted of the first offence, would have governed the court's power to quash that acquittal; but

    (3) for the requirement we propose at paragraph 5.38 above (namely that the new evidence must make the prosecution's case substantially stronger than it was at the first trial) should be substituted a requirement that the new evidence must substantially strengthen the evidence (if any) of the second offence that was in the possession of the prosecution at the time when the defendant was charged with the first offence.

    (paragraph 5.72)

THE TAINTED ACQUITTAL PROCEDURE

The objects of the interference or intimidation

14. We provisionally propose that the tainted acquittal procedure should be extended so as to apply where the administration of justice offence involves interference with, or intimidation of, a judge or magistrate.

    (paragraph 6.8)

The necessity for a conviction of an administration of justice offence

15. We invite views on whether the requirement that a person should have been convicted of an administration of justice offence should be

    (1) retained in all cases;

    (2) abolished and replaced with a requirement that the High Court should be satisfied (to the criminal standard of proof) that an administration of justice offence has been committed; or

    (3) retained except where it is impossible to try the person alleged to be guilty of the administration of justice offence, in which case the High Court should have to be satisfied (to the criminal standard of proof) that the offence has been committed.

We provisionally propose the second option.

    (paragraph 6.12)

16. We provisionally propose that, if the second or the third option in paragraph 15 above were adopted, the fact that the High Court has found that an administration of justice offence has been committed should not be admissible in any subsequent trial of a person for that offence or an offence arising out of the same or substantially the same facts as that offence.

(paragraph 6.13)

The requirement that the acquittal be secured by the interference or intimidation

17. We invite views on whether, when considering whether the acquittal was secured by the proven interference or intimidation, the High Court should apply

    (1)   the existing test (that this "appears to be likely");

    (2)   the civil standard of proof (that it is more likely than not);

    (3)   the criminal standard of proof (that the court is satisfied so that it is sure);

    (4)   the test applied by the Criminal Division of the Court of Appeal in deciding whether to quash a conviction on appeal (whether it is a "safe" conclusion); or

    (5)   some other test, and if so what.

(paragraph 6.17)

The definition of "administration of justice offence"

18. We invite views on whether, and if so how, the definition of an "administration of justice offence" should be extended.

(paragraph 6.21)

The interests of justice test

19. We provisionally propose that the interests of justice test be formulated in the same way as we have proposed in the case of new evidence.

(paragraph 6.22)

Additional safeguards

20. We invite views on whether the tainted acquittal procedure should be subject to a seriousness criterion, a limit to the number of times the procedure may be used, or a time limit.

(paragraph 6.24)

The procedure

21. We provisionally propose that provision be made

    (1) for a hearing of the question whether the acquittal should be quashed;

    (2) for the hearing to be in open court;

    (3) for the acquitted person to have a right to be present;

    (4) for both parties to be legally represented, and legal aid to be available for the acquitted person;

    (5) for witnesses to be heard and cross-examined on the question whether an administration of justice offence has been committed; and

    (6) for consideration of transcripts of the first trial, together with witnesses if necessary, in determining whether the acquitted person would not have been acquitted but for the interference or intimidation.

                                                                    (paragraph 6.41)

THE ROLE OF JUDICIAL DISCRETION

The *Connelly* principle

22. We provisionally propose that the *Connelly*[1] principle (namely that, where a person is charged with an offence which arises out of the same or substantially the same facts as another offence of which he or she has previously been acquitted or convicted, the court should stay the proceedings unless they are justified by special circumstances) should be wholly superseded by the extended rule against double jeopardy.

                                                                    (paragraph 7.5)

Abuse of process

23. We provisionally propose that a person whose acquittal is quashed under an exception to the rule against double jeopardy should not be precluded from applying for further proceedings to be stayed as an abuse of process.

                                                                    (paragraph 7.8)

THE RULE AGAINST CHALLENGING A PREVIOUS ACQUITTAL

24. We provisionally propose that

    (1) subject to the rule against double jeopardy and the rules on the admissibility of evidence of a defendant's previous misconduct, the rule in *Sambasivam*[2] (which prevents the prosecution from making an assertion

---

[1] *Connelly v DPP* [1964] AC 1254; see para 2.21 above.

[2] *Sambasivam v Public Prosecutor, Federation of Malaya* [1950] AC 458; see Part VIII above.

which is inconsistent with a previous acquittal of the defendant) should be abolished; and

(2)   if, contrary to our proposal, the rule is retained, it should not apply to an assertion supported by new evidence which could not with due diligence have been adduced at the first trial.

(paragraph 8.40)

ACQUITTAL AND CONVICTION

Delaying the point in proceedings at which the rule applies

25.   Our provisional view is that, for the purposes of the rule against double jeopardy and (if, contrary to the proposal at paragraph 24 above, it is retained) the rule in *Sambasivam*, a person should continue to be regarded as having been acquitted

(1)   where a jury return a verdict of not guilty, with or without consideration of the evidence; and

(2)   where the prosecution offers no evidence.

(paragraph 9.9)

Acquittal or conviction in another jurisdiction

26.   We invite views on whether the rule against double jeopardy and (if, contrary to the proposal at paragraph 24 above, it is retained) the rule in *Sambasivam* should apply

(1)   wherever the previous acquittal or conviction occurred;

(2)   unless the previous acquittal or conviction was in one of certain countries expressly excluded for this purpose;[3]

(3)   only if the previous acquittal or conviction was in a member state of the European Union; or

(4)   only if the previous acquittal or conviction was in England and Wales.[4]

We provisionally favour the first option.

(paragraph 9.15)

Extending the concept of an acquittal or conviction

27.   We invite views on whether, for the purposes of the rule against double jeopardy and (if, contrary to the proposal at paragraph 24 above, it is retained) the rule in

---

[3]   We would be grateful if anyone supporting this option could indicate how such an exceptional country could be identified.

[4]   We would be grateful if anyone supporting this option could indicate how acquittals and convictions in Scotland and Northern Ireland should be treated.

Sambasivam, any outcome of criminal proceedings which does not now count as an acquittal or conviction should count as such.

(paragraph 9.22)

RETROSPECTIVE EFFECT

28. We invite views as to whether, if our proposals were implemented, the legislation should apply to acquittals and convictions taking place before it comes into force.

(paragraph 10.16)

PROSECUTION APPEALS

29. If any respondents believe that the law of double jeopardy cannot sensibly be reformed without also rationalising the law relating to prosecution appeals, we invite views on how this might be done.

(paragraph 11.3)

APPENDIX A
EXTRACTS FROM RELEVANT LAW

CRIMINAL PROCEDURE AND INVESTIGATIONS ACT 1996

Section 54   Acquittals tainted by intimidation etc

(1)   This section applies where –

    (a)   a person has been acquitted of an offence, and

    (b)   a person has been convicted of an administration of justice offence involving interference with or intimidation of a juror or a witness (or potential witness) in any proceedings which led to the acquittal.

(2)   Where it appears to the court before which the person was convicted that –

    (a)   there is a real possibility that, but for the interference or intimidation, the acquitted person would not have been acquitted, and

    (b)   subsection (5) does not apply,

the court shall certify that it so appears.

(3)   Where a court certifies under subsection (2) an application may be made to the High Court for an order quashing the acquittal, and the Court shall make the order if (but shall not do so unless) the four conditions in section 55 are satisfied.

(4)   Where an order is made under subsection (3) proceedings may be taken against the acquitted person for the offence of which he was acquitted.

(5)   This subsection applies if, because of lapse of time or for any other reason, it would be contrary to the interests of justice to take proceedings against the acquitted person for the offence of which he was acquitted.

(6)   For the purposes of this section the following offences are administration of justice offences –

    (a)   the offence of perverting the course of justice;

    (b)   the offence under section 51(1) of the Criminal Justice and Public Order Act 1994 (intimidation etc of witnesses, jurors and others);

    (c)   an offence of aiding, abetting, counselling, procuring, suborning or inciting another person to commit an offence under section 1 of the Perjury Act 1911.

(7)   This section applies in relation to acquittals in respect of offences alleged to be committed on or after [15 April 1997].[1]

Section 55   Conditions for making order

(1)   The first condition is that it appears to the High Court likely that, but for the interference or intimidation, the acquitted person would not have been acquitted.

---

[1]   Criminal Procedure and Investigations Act 1996 (Appointed Day No 4) Order 1997, SI 1997 No 1019.

(2)   The second condition is that it does not appear to the Court that, because of lapse of time or for any other reason, it would be contrary to the interests of justice to take proceedings against the acquitted person for the offence of which he was acquitted.

(3)   The third condition is that it appears to the Court that the acquitted person has been given a reasonable opportunity to make written representations to the Court.

(4)   The fourth condition is that it appears to the Court that the conviction for the administration of justice offence will stand.

(5)   In applying subsection (4) the Court shall –

(a)   take into account all the information before it, but

(b)   ignore the possibility of new factors coming to light.

(6)   Accordingly, the fourth condition has the effect that the Court shall not make an order under section 54(3) if (for instance) it appears to the Court that any time allowed for giving notice of appeal has not expired or that an appeal is pending.

RULES OF THE SUPREME COURT, ORDER 116[2]

Application

1.   This Order shall apply in relation to acquittals in respect of offences alleged to be committed on or after 15th April 1997.

Interpretation

2.   In this Order, unless the context otherwise requires –

"the Act" means the Criminal Procedure and Investigations Act 1996;

"acquitted person" means a person whose acquittal of an offence is the subject of a certification under section 54(2) of the Act, and "acquittal" means the acquittal of that person of that offence;

"deponent" means a deponent to an affidavit filed under rule 5, 7, 8 or 9;

"magistrates' court" has the same meaning as in section 148 of the Magistrates' Courts Act 1980;

"prosecutor" means the individual or body which acted as prosecutor in the proceedings which led to the acquittal;

"record of court proceedings" means –

(a)   (where the proceedings took place in the Crown Court) a transcript of the evidence, or

(b)   a note of the evidence made by the justices' clerk,

in the proceedings which led to the conviction for the administration of justice offence referred to in section 54(1)(b) of the Act or, as the case may be, the proceedings which led to the acquittal;

"single judge" means a judge of the Queen's Bench Division.

---

[2]   Inserted by Rules of the Supreme Court (Amendment) 1998, SI 1998 No 1898.

Assignment of proceedings

3. The jurisdiction of the High Court under section 54(3) of the Act shall be exercised by a single judge and, subject to rule 10(13), that jurisdiction shall be exercised in chambers.

Time limit for making application

4. An application under section 54(3) of the Act shall be made not later than 28 days after –

   (a) the expiry of the period allowed for appealing (whether by case stated or otherwise), or making an application for leave to appeal, against the conviction referred to in section 54(1)(b) of the Act; or

   (b) where notice of appeal or application for leave to appeal against the conviction is given, the determination of the appeal or application for leave to appeal and, for this purpose, "determination" includes abandonment (within the meaning of rule 10 of the Criminal Appeal Rules 1968 or, as the case may be, rule 11 of the Crown Court Rules 1982).

Application

5(1) An application under section 54(3) of the Act shall be made by originating motion which shall be issued out of the Crown Office by the prosecutor.

(2) The application shall be accompanied by –

   (a) an affidavit which deals with the conditions in section 55(1), (2), and (4) of the Act and which exhibits any relevant documents (which may include a copy of any record of court proceedings);

   (b) a copy of the certification under section 54(2) of the Act.

Notice to the acquitted person

6(1) The prosecutor shall, within 4 days of the issue of the application, serve written notice on the acquitted person that the application has been issued.

(2) The notice given under paragraph (1) shall –

   (a) specify the date on which the application was issued;

   (b) be accompanied by a copy of the application and of the documents which accompanied it;

   (c) inform the acquitted person that –

      (i) the result of the application may be the making of an order by the High Court quashing the acquittal, and

      (ii) if he wishes to respond to the application, he must, within 28 days of the date of service on him of the notice, file in the Crown Office any affidavit on which he intends to rely.

Affidavit of service on an acquitted person

7. The prosecutor shall, as soon as practicable after service of the notice under rule 6, lodge with the Crown Office an affidavit of service which exhibits a copy of the notice.

Response of acquitted person

8(1) If the acquitted person wishes to respond to the application, he shall, within 28 days of service on him of notice under rule 6, file in the Crown Office an affidavit which –

    (a) deals with the conditions in section 55(1), (2), and (4) of the Act; and

    (b) exhibits any relevant documents (which may include a copy of any record of court proceedings).

(2) The acquitted person shall, within 4 days of the filing of the documents mentioned in paragraph (1), serve copies of them on the prosecutor.

Evidence

9(1) An affidavit filed under rule 5, 7, 8 or this rule may contain statements of information or belief with the sources and grounds thereof.

(2) The prosecutor may, not later than 10 days after expiry of the period allowed under rule 8(1), apply ex parte for an order granting leave to file further affidavit evidence.

(3) If the single judge grants leave, the order shall specify a period within which further affidavit evidence or records are to be filed, and the Crown Office shall serve a copy of the order on the prosecutor and on the acquitted person.

(4) The prosecutor shall, within 4 days of filing further evidence in the Crown Office, serve a copy of that evidence on the acquitted person.

Determination of the application

10(1) Subject to paragraph (3), the single judge shall determine whether or not to make an order under section 54(3) of the Act on the basis of the written material provided under rules 5, 7, 8 and 9 in the absence of the prosecutor, the acquitted person, or of any deponent.

(2) The determination shall not be made, and any hearing under paragraph (3) shall not take place, before the expiry of –

    (a) 10 days after the expiry of the period allowed under rule 8(1), or

    (b) 10 days after the expiry of the period allowed by any order made under rule 9(3).

(3) The single judge may, of his own motion or on the application of the prosecutor or acquitted person, order a hearing of the application if he thinks fit.

(4) An application under paragraph (3) shall state whether a hearing is desired in order for a deponent for the other party to attend and be cross-examined, and, if so, the reasons for wishing the deponent to attend.

(5) An application under paragraph (3) shall be made no later than 7 days after the expiry of the period allowed –

    (a) under rule 8(1) or

    (b) by any order made under rule 9(3).

(6) Where a hearing is ordered, the single judge may, of his own motion or on the application of the prosecutor or acquitted person, order a deponent to attend in order to be cross-examined.

(7)   The prosecutor or the acquitted person, as the case may be, shall within 4 days after lodging the application under paragraph (3), serve a copy of it on the other party, and file in the Crown Office an affidavit of service.

(8)   A party served under paragraph (7) shall, within 5 days of service, file any representations he wishes to make as to whether or not a hearing should be ordered.

(9)   Subject to paragraph (10) below –

    (a)   the single judge shall not determine an application for a hearing under paragraph (3) unless –

        (i)   an affidavit of service has been filed as required by paragraph (7), and

        (ii)   the period for filing representations allowed under paragraph (8) has elapsed; or

        (iii)   representations have been filed under paragraph (8).

    (b)   The requirements imposed by sub-paragraph (a)(i) and (iii) are satisfied even though the affidavit of service or, as the case may be, the representations are filed outside the time limits allowed.

(10)   Where after an application for a hearing has been made –

    (a)   no affidavit of service has been filed and

    (b)   no representations under paragraph (8) have been received after the expiry of 7 days from the lodging of the application,

the single judge may reject the application.

(11)   Where after a hearing is ordered, either the prosecutor or the acquitted person desires a deponent for the other party to attend the hearing in order to be cross-examined, he must apply ex parte, for an order under paragraph (5) giving his reasons.

(12)   The Crown Office shall serve notice on the prosecutor and the acquitted person of any order made under the foregoing paragraphs of this rule and, where a hearing is ordered, the notice shall –

    (a)   set out the date, time and place of the hearing, and

    (b)   give details of any deponent ordered to attend for cross-examination.

(13)   A hearing ordered under paragraph (3) above shall be in open court unless the single judge otherwise directs.

(14)   The Crown Office shall serve notice of any order made under section 54(3) of the Act quashing the acquittal or of a decision not to make such an order on the prosecutor, the acquitted person and –

    (a)   where the court before which the acquittal or conviction occurred was a magistrates' court, on the justices' clerk;

    (b)   where the court before which the acquittal or conviction occurred was the Crown Court, on the appropriate officer of the Crown Court sitting at the place where the acquittal or conviction occurred.

THE EUROPEAN CONVENTION ON HUMAN RIGHTS

Article 6: Right to a fair trial

1.   In the determination of his civil rights and obligations or of any criminal charge against him, everyone is entitled to a fair and public hearing within a reasonable time by an independent and impartial tribunal established by law. Judgment shall be pronounced publicly but the press and public may be excluded from all or part of the trial in the interests of morals, public order or national security in a democratic society, where the interests of juveniles or the protection of the private life of the parties so require, or to the extent strictly necessary in the opinion of the court in special circumstances where publicity would prejudice the interests of justice.

2.   Everyone charged with a criminal offence shall be presumed innocent until proved guilty according to law.

3.   Everyone charged with a criminal offence has the following minimum rights:

   (a)   to be informed promptly, in a language which he understands and in detail, of the nature and cause of the accusation against him;

   (b)   to have adequate time and facilities for the preparation of his defence;

   (c)   to defend himself in person or through legal assistance of his own choosing or, if he has not sufficient means to pay for legal assistance, to be given it free when the interests of justice so require;

   (d)   to examine or have examined witnesses against him and to obtain the attendance and examination of witnesses on his behalf under the same conditions as witnesses against him;

   (e)   to have the free assistance of an interpreter if he cannot understand or speak the language used in court.

Article 7: No punishment without law

1.   No one shall be held guilty of any criminal offence on account of any act or omission which did not constitute a criminal offence under national or international law at the time when it was committed. Nor shall a heavier penalty be imposed than the one that was applicable at the time the criminal offence was committed.

2.   This article shall not prejudice the trial and punishment of any person for any act or omission which, at the time when it was committed, was criminal according to the general principles of law recognised by civilised nations.

Article 4 of Protocol 7: Right not to be tried or punished twice

1.   No one shall be liable to be tried or punished again in criminal proceedings under the jurisdiction of the same State for an offence for which he has already been finally acquitted or convicted in accordance with the law and penal procedure of that State.

2.   The provisions of the preceding paragraph shall not prevent the reopening of the case in accordance with the law and penal procedure of the State concerned, if there is evidence of new or newly discovered facts, or if there has been a fundamental defect in the previous proceedings, which could affect the outcome of the case.

3.   No derogation from this Article shall be made under Article 15 of the Convention.

26   This Article embodies the principle that a person may not be tried or punished again in criminal proceedings under the jurisdiction of the same State for an offence for which he has already been finally acquitted or convicted (*non bis in idem*).

27   The words "under the jurisdiction of the same State" limit the application of the Article to the national level. Several other Council of Europe Conventions, including the European Convention on Extradition (1957), the European Convention on the International Validity of Criminal Judgments (1970) and the European Convention on the Transfer of Proceedings in Criminal Matters (1972), govern the application of the principle at the international level.

28   It has not seemed necessary, as in Articles 2 and 3 to qualify the offence as "criminal". Indeed, Article 4 already contains the terms "in criminal proceedings" and "penal procedure", which render unnecessary any further specification in the text of the Article itself.

29   The principle established in this provision applies only after the person has been finally acquitted or convicted in accordance with the law and penal procedure of the State concerned. This means that there must have been a final decision as defined above, in paragraph 22.[3]

30   A case may, however, be reopened in accordance with the law of the State concerned if there is evidence of new or newly discovered facts, or if it appears that there has been a fundamental defect in the proceedings, which could affect the outcome of the case either in favour of the person or to his detriment.

31   The term "new or newly discovered facts" includes new means of proof relating to previously existing facts. Furthermore, this Article does not prevent a reopening of the proceedings in favour of the convicted person and any other changing of the judgment to the benefit of the convicted person.

32   Article 4, since it only applies to trial and conviction of a person in criminal proceedings, does not prevent him from being made subject, for the same act, to action of a different character (for example disciplinary action in the case of an official) as well as to criminal proceedings.

33   Under the terms of paragraph 3, this Article may not be subject to derogation under Article 15 of the Convention in time of war or other public emergency threatening the life of the nation.

---

[3]   In relation to Article 3 of Protocol No 7 (compensation for wrongful conviction), paragraph 22 of the Explanatory Report reads as follows:

> According to the definition contained in the explanatory report of the European Convention on the International Validity of Criminal Judgments, a decision is final "if, according to the traditional expression, it has acquired the force of res judicata. This is the case when it is irrevocable, that is to say when no further ordinary remedies are available or when the parties have exhausted such remedies or have permitted the time-limit to expire without availing themselves of them". It follows therefore that a judgment by default is not considered as final as long as the domestic law allows the proceedings to be taken up again. Likewise this Article does not apply in cases where the charge is dismissed or the accused person is acquitted either by the court of first instance or, on appeal, by a higher tribunal. If, however, in one of the States in which such a possibility is provided for, the person has been granted leave to appeal after the normal time of appealing has expired, and his conviction is then reversed on appeal, then ... the Article may apply.

APPENDIX B
THE LAW OF DOUBLE JEOPARDY IN OTHER JURISDICTIONS

AUSTRALIA

B.1 All the Australian states and territories (including those that do not have a criminal code) have legislation which enshrines the rule against double jeopardy. As in England and Wales,[1] the strict autrefois rule normally applies only where an acquitted or convicted person is charged again with the same offence.[2] Where a person has previously been acquitted or convicted of an offence and is later charged with a *different* offence arising out of the same or substantially the same facts, the plea of autrefois is not available[3] but the second proceedings may be stayed as an abuse of process.[4] The Supreme Court of Tasmania has adopted the approach laid down by Lord Devlin in *Connelly*[5] and applied by the Court of Appeal in *Beedie*,[6] namely that in a case of the latter type the proceedings should be stayed unless they are justified by special circumstances.[7] But the High Court of Australia has preferred a more flexible approach, involving the balancing of a variety of considerations including the need for fairness to the accused, the legitimate public interest in the disposition of charges of serious offences and in the conviction of those guilty of crime, and the need to maintain public confidence in the administration of justice.[8]

B.2 In all the states and territories the prosecution may challenge an error of law by a court of summary jurisdiction, usually (as in England and Wales) by way of case stated.[9] In South Australia, however, the prosecution may also appeal to the Supreme Court against a judgment dismissing a charge of a summary or minor indictable offence.[10] This right of appeal is not limited to questions of law; and the Supreme Court can make any order that may be necessary or desirable in the

---

[1] *Connelly v DPP* [1964] AC 1254; see para 2.4 above.

[2] *Pearce* [1998] HCA 57. But s 18 of the Criminal Code of the Northern Territory extends the rule to the case where the second charge is of "a similar offence" to the first. A similar offence is defined as "an offence in which the conduct therein impugned is substantially the same as or includes the conduct impugned in the offence to which it is said to be similar": s 17. But an acquittal or conviction of a "regulatory" offence does not bar a subsequent prosecution for a more serious offence: s 20.

[3] Except in the Northern Territory: see n 2 above.

[4] *Rogers* (1994) 181 CLR 251; *Pearce* [1998] HCA 57.

[5] [1964] AC 1254, 1359–1360; see para 2.21 above.

[6] [1998] QB 356; see para 2.22 above.

[7] *Hutton* (1992) 3 Tas R 225.

[8] *Rogers* (1994) 181 CLR 251; *Pearce* [1998] HCA 57.

[9] Eg Justices Act 1902 (NSW) s 101.

[10] Magistrates' Courts Act 1991 (SA) s 42(1).

circumstances. This includes quashing the judgment and remitting the case to the magistrates' court for further hearing.

B.3 In general the prosecution has no right of appeal against an acquittal on indictment, but there are statutory exceptions to this rule in Tasmania and Western Australia. In Tasmania the Attorney-General may appeal against an acquittal, provided that the Supreme Court gives leave or the trial judge certifies that it is a fit case for appeal.[11] But this right of appeal appears to extend only to pure questions of law, not questions of mixed fact and law.[12]

B.4 The Supreme Court may set aside the acquittal, and order a new trial or enter a conviction,

> if it is of the opinion that the verdict of the jury should be set aside on the ground that it is unreasonable, or cannot be supported having regard to the evidence, or that the judgment or order of the court of trial should be set aside on the ground of the wrong decision of any question of law, or that on any ground whatsoever there was a miscarriage of justice ... .[13]

B.5 Similarly, in Western Australia the prosecution has a right of appeal against an acquittal on the direction of the judge.[14] The Court of Criminal Appeal can reverse the verdict or order a new trial.[15]

B.6 In all states the Crown can submit a question of law to the appeal court where the defendant has been acquitted, but the determination of the question does not affect the acquittal. The question of double jeopardy therefore does not arise.

---

[11] Criminal Code Act 1924 (Tas) s 401(2)(b).

[12] *Jenkins* [1970] Tas SR 13; *Williams* (1986) 161 CLR 278. Section 401(2)(b) originally referred to "any question of law alone", and the word "alone" was deleted by the Criminal Code Amendment Act 1987, s 7. Arguably the effect of this amendment is to allow an appeal on a question of mixed fact and law. But the New South Wales Law Reform Commission has rejected this suggestion, on the ground that the word "alone" was also removed from s 401(1)(a), which confers a right of appeal against *conviction* on a question of law; and appeals against conviction on questions of mixed fact and law are governed not by that provision but by s 401(1)(b). Discussion Paper No 37, *Directed Verdicts of Acquittal* (1995) p 18.

[13] Criminal Code Act 1924, s 402(1).

[14] Criminal Code Act 1913, s 688(2)(b). The section also provides for a right of appeal against a verdict of acquittal by a judge without a jury, under provisions which allow a person charged with an indictable offence to elect to be tried by a judge alone.

[15] *Ibid*, s 690(3).

B.7　Section 26(2) of the New Zealand Bill of Rights 1990 provides that "No one who has been finally acquitted or convicted of, or pardoned for, an offence shall be tried or punished for it again." This general principle is implemented by sections 358 and 359 of the Crimes Act 1961.[16] Section 358(1) provides as follows:

> On the trial of an issue on a plea of previous acquittal or conviction to any count, if it appears that the matter on which the accused was formerly charged is the same in whole or in part as that on which it is proposed to give him in charge, and that he might on the former trial, if all proper amendments had been made that might then have been made, have been convicted of all the offences of which he may be convicted on any count to which that plea is pleaded, the Court shall give judgment that he be discharged from that count.[17]

B.8　Thus the defendant can plead the previous acquittal or conviction even if he or she could not have been convicted of the offence now charged on the previous indictment *as it was*, provided that the indictment could have been *amended* so as to make such a conviction possible. The underlying policy is that all offences arising out of a particular incident should if possible be dealt with in one trial. The defendant is protected against double jeopardy if it is attributable solely to the prosecution's failure to lay an appropriately drafted indictment. This approach is similar to that adopted by Lord Devlin in *Connelly*[18] and applied by the Court of Appeal in *Beedie*;[19] but, unlike Lord Devlin's principle, section 358(1) applies only where the present charge is "the same in whole or in part" as the previous one. Thus it did not apply where the defendant was acquitted of driving a motor vehicle with excess breath alcohol and later charged, in relation to the same incident, with driving while under the influence of drink or drug so as to be incapable of having proper control. The former charge was not the same, in whole or in part, as the latter.[20]

B.9　Section 359(1) extends the plea of previous acquittal or conviction to cases where the defendant could not have been convicted at the earlier trial of the offence now charged, but the later charge is in substance an aggravated version of the earlier one. It provides as follows:

---

[16]　Sections 358 and 359 apply both to trial on indictment and to summary proceedings, whether in respect of summary offences or in respect of indictable offences dealt with summarily: Summary Proceedings Act 1957, s 3(1)(j).

[17]　Section 358(2) adds:

> If it appears that the accused might on the former trial have been convicted of any offence of which he might be convicted on the count to which that plea [of previous acquittal] is pleaded, but that he may be convicted on that count of some offence of which he could not have been convicted on the former trial, the Court shall direct that he shall not be convicted on that count of any offence of which he might have been convicted on the former trial, but that he shall plead over as to any other offence charged.

[18]　[1964] AC 1254, 1359–1360; see para 2.21 above.

[19]　[1998] QB 356; see para 2.22 above.

[20]　*Ministry of Transport v Hyndman* [1990] 3 NZLR 480.

Where an indictment charges substantially the same offence as that with which the accused was formerly charged, but adds a statement of intention or circumstances of aggravation tending if proved to increase the punishment, the previous acquittal or conviction shall be a bar to the indictment.

Thus a conviction for possession of a prohibited drug was a bar to a later indictment for possession of the drug for the purpose of selling it to others.[21] The determination of whether the charges are substantially the same for the purposes of section 359(1) does not depend solely upon a technical or formal comparison of the elements of the two charges. It is a matter of substance rather than form.[22]

B.10   It was held in *Moevao v Department of Labour*[23] that the superior courts, at least,[24] have an inherent jurisdiction to stay proceedings which are an abuse of process. The arguments of Lords Devlin and Pearce in *Connelly v DPP*[25] were adopted. Although *Connelly* was itself a double jeopardy case, it is not clear whether this jurisdiction might be invoked on grounds of double jeopardy in a case falling outside sections 358 and 359 of the Crimes Act 1961.

CANADA

B.11   Section 11(h) of the Canadian Charter of Rights and Freedoms provides that any person charged with an offence has the right

if finally acquitted of the offence, not to be tried for it again and, if finally found guilty and punished for the offence, not to be tried or punished for it again.

The Charter of Rights and Freedoms is incorporated within the Canadian constitution by section 52(2) of the Constitution Act 1982.

B.12   Section 11(h) appears to protect the defendant only from being prosecuted again for exactly the same offence as before.[26] However, the Canadian Criminal Code provides substantially greater protection. Section 607(1)(a) of the Code provides that an accused may plead autrefois acquit or autrefois convict. These pleas are

---

[21]   *Lee* [1973] NZLR 13.

[22]   *R Pene* [1982] 2 NZLR 652.

[23]   [1980] 1 NZLR 464.

[24]   Only Woodhouse J expressed the view that *every* criminal court has such a jurisdiction: [1980] 1 NZLR 464, 476. In *Department of Social Welfare v Stewart* [1990] 1 NZLR 697, however, it was held that the District Court, a court of summary jurisdiction, had an inherent power to dismiss an information on the ground of delay. Wylie J, giving judgment, observed at p 706 that "the categories of abuse of process are never closed", and thought it clear that the District Court has an inherent power to prevent an abuse of process.

[25]   [1964] AC 1254.

[26]   Tarnopolsky and Beaudoin, *Canadian Charter of Rights and Freedoms: Commentary* (1982) p 384.

available in summary proceedings as well as trial on indictment.[27] Section 609(1) provides:

> Where an issue on a plea of autrefois acquit or autrefois convict to a count is tried and it appears
>
> > (a)   that the matter on which the accused was given in charge on the former trial is the same in whole or in part as that on which it is proposed to give him in charge, and
> >
> > (b)   that on the former trial, if all proper amendments had been made that might then have been made, he might have been convicted of all the offences of which he may be convicted on the count to which the plea of autrefois acquit or autrefois convict is pleaded,
>
> the judge shall give judgment discharging the accused in respect of that count.

B.13   For section 609(1) to bite, the offence charged need not be exactly the same as the one of which the defendant has previously been acquitted or convicted; but it must be "the same in whole or in part". In *Van Rassel*[28] the defendant was a constable in the Royal Canadian Mounted Police. He was charged in the USA with soliciting and accepting bribes, but was acquitted. He was later charged in Canada with committing a breach of trust in connection with his duties as a Canadian official. It was held that section 609(1) did not apply because he could not have been convicted on the American charges of the offences with which he was charged in Canada.

B.14   Section 609(1) is almost identical to section 358(1) of the New Zealand Crimes Act,[29] and reflects a similar policy. By extending the plea to a defendant who could previously have been convicted of the offence now charged "if all proper amendments had been made that might then have been made", section 609(1) "protects the accused from a second trial being necessitated by lack of diligence on the part of the Crown."[30] Similarly, section 610(1) of the Canadian Code corresponds to section 359(1) of the New Zealand Crimes Act,[31] and protects a defendant against being charged with an aggravated form of an offence for which he or she has previously been tried.

B.15   Section 676(1) of the Criminal Code gives the Attorney General a limited right of appeal against an acquittal on indictment. It provides:

> The Attorney General or counsel instructed by him for the purpose may appeal to the court of appeal

---

[27]   *Riddle* [1980] 1 SCR 380.

[28]   [1990] 1 SCR 225.

[29]   See para B.7 above.

[30]   Del Buono (ed), *Criminal Procedure in Canada* (1982) p 250.

[31]   See para B.9 above.

(a) against a judgment or verdict of acquittal or a verdict of not criminally responsible on account of mental disorder of a trial court in proceedings by indictment on any ground of appeal that involves a question of law alone;

(b) against an order of a superior court of criminal jurisdiction that quashes an indictment or in any manner refuses or fails to exercise jurisdiction on an indictment;

(c) against an order of a trial court that stays proceedings on an indictment or quashes an indictment.

B.16 The words "a question of law alone" in section 676(1)(a) mean that the ground for appeal must not involve the weighing of evidence by the appellate court.[32] But there may be a question of law alone if the appeal could be allowed without the appellate court trespassing on the fact-finding function of the trial judge. The Supreme Court of Canada has said that there are three situations in which this may be so, namely where the trial judge

(1) fails to appreciate the legal effect of undisputed facts;

(2) owing to the misapprehension of some legal principle, fails to appreciate the evidence; or

(3) fails to apply the criminal standard to the totality of the evidence.[33]

B.17 Section 686(4) provides that, where an appeal against an acquittal is allowed, the court of appeal may set aside the verdict and order a new trial. Alternatively it may enter a verdict of guilty, but not if the appeal is from the verdict of a jury. It may also make any additional order that justice requires.[34]

B.18 In certain circumstances a defendant whose acquittal is set aside may appeal to the Supreme Court of Canada. Section 691(2) provides:

A person who is acquitted of an indictable offence other than by reason of a verdict of not criminally responsible on account of mental disorder and whose acquittal is set aside by the court of appeal may appeal to the Supreme Court of Canada

(a) on any question of law on which a judge of the court of appeal dissents;

(b) on any question of law, if the Court of Appeal enters a verdict of guilty against the person; or

---

[32] *Poirer* (1997) 147 Nfld & PEIR 195.

[33] *Morin* [1992] 3 SCR 286.

[34] Section 686(8).

(c)   on any question of law, if leave to appeal is granted by the Supreme Court of Canada.

Thus the defendant has no *right* of appeal, but must seek the leave of the Supreme Court, if the appellate court unanimously sets aside the acquittal and orders a new trial (as distinct from substituting a conviction, which under section 686(4) it cannot do if the acquittal was by the verdict of a jury).

B.19   In the case of a *summary* acquittal the prosecutor has a right of appeal under section 813. Leave is not required, and the appeal may be on a question of fact rather than law. Alternatively, there is a right of appeal under section 830 on a point of law or on jurisdictional grounds.

Abuse of process

B.20   The law of Canada recognises the doctrine of abuse of process, and the inherent power of the courts to protect judicial proceedings from such abuse. Moreover, section 7 of the Charter of Rights and Freedoms provides:

> Everyone has the right to life, liberty and security of the person and the right not to be deprived thereof except in accordance with the principles of fundamental justice.

The expression "fundamental justice" refers to the right of citizens in a free and democratic society to a fair procedure.[35] There is therefore a substantial overlap between section 7 of the Charter and the common law doctrine.[36]

Issue estoppel

B.21   In *Gushue*[37] the Supreme Court recognised issue estoppel as part of the criminal law of Canada, and expressed the view that "there are thin but nonetheless discernible lines between issue estoppel and inconsistent verdicts and double jeopardy."[38] It referred to the "initial difficulty in giving effect to a plea of issue estoppel where it is directed to the verdict of a jury which consists either of a bare finding of guilty or one of not guilty",[39] and adopted the test put forward by Friedland:

> The possibility or even the probability that the jury found in the accused's favour on a particular issue is not enough. A finding on the relevant issue must be the only rational explanation of the verdict of the jury.[40]

[35]   *Re Potma* (1983) 2 CCC (3d) 383, 391–392.

[36]   *O'Connor* [1995] 4 SCR 411.

[37]   [1980] 1 SCR 798.

[38]   [1980] 1 SCR 798, 802.

[39]   [1980] 1 SCR 798, 803.

[40]   *Double Jeopardy* (1969) p 134.

SCOTLAND[41]

B.22 The law of double jeopardy in Scotland is broadly similar to that in England and Wales. An accused person at risk of double jeopardy may plead res judicata. A verdict of not proven is a verdict of acquittal, and is therefore a bar to further proceedings.

B.23 As in England and Wales, a person who has previously been tried for an offence may be tried for an aggravated form of that offence if the circumstances of aggravation arose after the first trial. Thus a defendant previously convicted of assault may be tried for homicide if the victim's death later results.[42]

B.24 Also, the High Court may grant authority to bring a new prosecution where it quashes a conviction on appeal.[43] The accused may then be charged with the same or any similar offence arising out of the same facts, and the proceedings out of which the appeal arose are not a bar to the new prosecution.[44]

B.25 The prosecution has no right of appeal against the verdict of a jury.[45] Where a person tried on indictment is acquitted of a charge, the Lord Advocate may refer to the High Court a point of law which has arisen in relation to that charge;[46] but the High Court's opinion does not affect the acquittal.[47]

B.26 Where a person has been acquitted in *summary* proceedings, section 175(3) of the Criminal Procedure (Scotland) Act 1995 allows the prosecutor to appeal to the High Court by stated case, on a point of law. Where an appeal under section 175 would be incompetent or inappropriate, section 191(1) allows the prosecutor to appeal by bill of advocation, "on the ground of an alleged miscarriage of justice in the proceedings". The common law rule is that advocation is not available to review the merits of a case;[48] but it has been suggested that this must be qualified by section 191(1) because advocation is expressly made available where a stated case is not.[49] Advocation is not available in the case of an acquittal by a jury, whether or not at the direction of the judge.[50]

---

[41] We are grateful for the assistance of the Scottish Law Commission with this section.

[42] *Tees v HM Advocate* 1994 SLT 701.

[43] Criminal Procedure (Scotland) Act 1995, s 118(1)(c).

[44] *Ibid*, s 119(1). As in England and Wales, the new prosecution may not be for a more serious offence than the one of which the accused was convicted: s 119(2). In this respect the 1995 Act reverses the previous position. In *HM Advocate v Boyle* 1992 SCCR 939 the accused had been charged with murder, but convicted only of culpable homicide. On appeal, the verdict was set aside and a new prosecution authorised. It was held that the new prosecution could include the charge of murder, of which the jury's verdict had impliedly acquitted him, because, having been set aside, the verdict had to be entirely disregarded.

[45] The Laws of Scotland, Stair Memorial Encyclopaedia, vol 17, para 814.

[46] Criminal Procedure (Scotland) Act 1995, s 123(1).

[47] *Ibid*, s 123(5).

[48] *McLeod v Levitt* 1969 JC 16.

[49] *Renton and Brown's Criminal Procedure* (6th ed 1996) para 33-29.

[50] *Ibid*, para 33-30.

B.27 There are two forms of appeal. An appeal on both fact and law is admissible against a finding of the court which tries less serious crime (the Amtsgericht);[52] and an appeal on the law only is available generally.[53] The prosecution may use either form of appeal against an acquittal.[54] A verdict becomes final when the time allowed to file an appeal elapses.

B.28 An acquittal can be reopened after it has become final, if

(1) a document presented as genuine at the trial was fake or forged;

(2) a witness or an expert has given false evidence, and committed an offence in so doing;

(3) a judge or lay-judge involved in the trial has committed a criminal offence relating to his or her duty in relation to the trial; or

(4) the defendant has made a credible confession.[55]

B.29 Under the second and third heads, a crime must have been committed. An application under the first head may be on the basis that a crime was committed, or on the merely mistaken tendering of a fake or forged document. Where reliance is placed on the committing of a crime, there must either be a final conviction in the matter or the initiation of criminal proceedings must be impossible for some reason other than lack of evidence.[56]

B.30 The procedure is for a motion to be brought before a court within the same state and of the same jurisdictional level as that before which the defendant was originally acquitted. A particular court is nominated in advance to deal with the motions. There is a three stage process.[57] The court first determines whether the motion is "permissible" – that is, whether the motion is in the proper form, and contains proper grounds for reopening and suitable proof of the grounds.[58] There is no oral hearing at this stage.[59]

---

[51] We are grateful for the assistance of Christiane Rabenstein with this section.

[52] German Code of Criminal Procedure, ss 312–332.

[53] *Ibid*, ss 333–358.

[54] *Ibid*, s 296.

[55] *Ibid*, s 362.

[56] *Ibid*, s 364. See also J Hatchard, B Huber and R Vogler, *Comparative Criminal Procedure* (1996) p 135.

[57] Criminal Justice Systems in Other Jurisdictions, Royal Commission on Criminal Justice research paper (1993) p 102. The account in the paper is largely limited to reopening at the instance of the defendant, but the procedural requirements are the same (German Code of Criminal Procedure, ss 365-370).

[58] German Code of Criminal Procedure, s 368.

[59] *Ibid*, s 367 II. Section 367 I states: "The court whose judgment is attacked by the motion decides with respect to the permissibility of the motion for reopening".

B.31   The second stage is the substantive determination of the motion. At this stage, witnesses are examined in the presence of the prosecution and defence counsel. The defendant, if in custody, has only a limited right to be present. It is a matter for the discretion of the court whether the witnesses are sworn. If the motion is successful, a new trial takes place (the third stage).[60]

BELGIUM

B.32   In Belgium, both the prosecution and the defence can appeal against verdicts in most courts,[61] using either a procedure by which questions of both law and fact can be raised, or a cassation procedure relating only to points of law. There is also a separate procedure by which a party who was absent (ie the defendant or a civil party) may challenge a judgment. A final judgment, however, can only be reopened in favour of the defendant.[62]

THE NETHERLANDS[63]

B.33   Both the prosecution and the defendant have an ordinary right of appeal. Appeals against decisions by a sub-district court (which tries less serious misdemeanours) must be lodged with the district court, and appeals against decisions of a district court (which tries more serious crimes, and is composed of three members) with a court of appeal. An appeal in the Netherlands involves a complete retrial by the higher judicial authority. There is an additional safeguard where the prosecution appeals against an acquittal, however, in that the defendant can only be convicted on appeal if the court is unanimous.[64]

B.34   There is a further appeal to the Supreme Court, on a point of law alone, against decisions rendered on appeal. Although the prosecution may appeal to the Supreme Court against other decisions, this avenue of appeal is not available against an acquittal. If it concludes that the appeal is well-founded, the Supreme Court usually refers the case back to the lower courts.[65]

B.35   There is provision for a final judgment to be revised where contradictory verdicts have been reached, or if new facts have emerged which cast serious doubt on a conviction. It is not enough for the court to have made an error of law, or for

---

[60]   *Ibid*, ss 369, 370. There is no further oral hearing over and above the examination of witnesses by the responsible judge at the second stage: s 370.

[61]   The principal exception being verdicts of an assize court, in which guilt is determined by a jury. Originally, all *crime*, or offences punishable by five or more years' imprisonment, were tried in these courts. However, their role is now restricted to the most serious offences: Christine Van den Wyngaert (ed) *Criminal Procedure Systems in the European Community* (1993) pp 10–12.

[62]   *Ibid*, pp 45–48.

[63]   We are grateful for the assistance of Dr G J M Corstens with this section.

[64]   Van den Wyngaert, *op cit*, pp 287, 314.

[65]   *Ibid*, p 314.

legislation or case law to have changed. Reopening is available only to the defendant.[66]

ITALY

B.36 All parties, including the prosecution, have a right of appeal to the Court of Appeal, on questions of fact or law, and without leave.[67] However, the limited remedy of revision, by which a case can be reopened and retried following final judgment, applies to convictions only.[68]

SPAIN[69]

B.37 In Spain, there is a procedural distinction between petty offences and offences punishable by five years' imprisonment or less, which are tried by a single investigating judge,[70] and more serious offences, which go before a Provincial Criminal Court of three members. Both the prosecution and the defence may appeal on matters of fact or law against a conviction for a less serious offence, but only an appeal in cassation, on a point of law, is available (to either party) in respect of the most serious category.[71] There is also provision for challenges against the orders concluding the investigative stage.[72]

B.38 There is an extraordinary procedure for challenging a final verdict, essentially on the basis of new evidence (although there is some scope for a challenge on narrow points of law), but it applies only to convictions.[73]

DENMARK

B.39 The attorney general may petition a special court of complaint for a retrial, where a defendant has been acquitted or convicted of a lesser offence. The procedure is available if either the defendant makes a later confession, or there is strong new evidence; or where the verdict was the result of a crime, including an offence committed by a participant in the trial.[74]

---

[66] *Ibid*, p 315.

[67] Royal Commission on Criminal Justice, *Criminal Justice Systems in other Jurisdictions* (1993) para 10.45.

[68] Van den Wyngaert, *op cit*, p 257.

[69] We are grateful for the assistance of Enrique Bacigalupo Zapater with this section.

[70] Or, in the case of the most minor petty offences, a justice of the peace.

[71] Van den Wyngaert, *op cit*, pp 387, 397–398.

[72] *Ibid*, p 395.

[73] *Ibid*, p 398; Spanish Code of Criminal Procedure, Art 954.

[74] Administration of Justice Act 1916, s 976. The Court of Complaints is appointed for a ten year period, and is composed of one judge each from the Supreme Court, the high courts, and the City courts, a defence counsel and an academic lawyer: Van den Wyngaert, *op cit*, p 71.

B.40   The procedure is rarely used in practice, and then usually only on the ground that the defendant has made a confession. There is a similar procedure for the reopening of a conviction, in respect of which the criteria are less strict.[75]

FINLAND

B.41   A final acquittal may be annulled, and a new trial ordered, if it was the result of a criminal act of the judge or of the parties; or if new evidence surfaces after the trial which, had it been available at the time of the trial, would in all likelihood have led to a conviction. This procedure is available only if the offence is punishable with at least two years' imprisonment. Where new evidence is relied on, the acquittal can be annulled only if the failure to present the evidence at the first trial was not due to negligence.

B.42   A petition for the annulment of a trial must be lodged with the Supreme Court within one year of the discovery of the new evidence or from the date when criminal liability of the judge or other party was established. Apart from this, there is no other time limit.[76]

B.43   The procedure is very rarely used.[77]

---

[75]   Lars Bo Langsted, Vagn Greve and Peter Garde, *Criminal Law in Denmark* (1998) pp 194–195.

[76]   Criminal Procedure Act, ch 31, s 9.

[77]   Information from the Finnish Ministry of Justice.

APPENDIX C
SENTENCING PRACTICE

C.1 In Part V we proposed that the rule against double jeopardy should be subject to an exception in certain cases where new evidence emerges. One of the conditions to which we proposed that this exception should be subject is that the offence to be charged would be likely to attract a sentence of a specified minimum severity.[1] In order to help respondents form a view on what would be an appropriate minimum sentence for this purpose, in this appendix we give a broad indication of the kinds of sentence that various kinds of crime are likely to attract.

C.2 One option would be to make the new exception applicable to any offence for which the defendant would be likely to receive a custodial sentence. We therefore begin by setting out what is said in the Magistrates' Association's Sentencing Guidelines[2] on the point at which imprisonment becomes appropriate.

C.3 An alternative option would be to confine the new exception to cases where, if convicted, the defendant could expect to be imprisoned for a certain minimum period.[3] We therefore give illustrations of the periods of imprisonment that are currently regarded by the courts as appropriate for various kinds of crime. In the case of each broad category of crime, we refer first to any cases in which the Court of Appeal has laid down guidelines for use by sentencers, followed by a number of illustrative cases. The information in this section comes from *Current Sentencing Practice*.[4]

DETERMINING WHETHER TO IMPOSE A SENTENCE OF IMPRISONMENT

C.4 The Magistrates' Association's guidelines are a way of assisting magistrates in the sentencing process. They do not provide a "tariff" for each offence. In respect of offences commonly encountered in the adult magistrates' court, the guidelines set down as a starting point the "seriousness category" appropriate for a case of average seriousness. The categories are, first, discharge, compensation or fine; secondly, community penalty; and finally, custody.[5] The guidelines then set out examples of aggravating and mitigating features relating to the offence itself, and mitigating features relating to the offender personally, which the magistrates should consider before coming to a final decision.

C.5 Custody is the starting point for the following offences: affray; aggravated vehicle taking; assault occasioning actual bodily harm; assault on a police officer; burglary of a dwelling house; the production or supply of a class A drug; possession with intent to supply a class B drug; causing harassment, alarm or distress with intent;

---

[1]   See para 5.27 above.

[2]   1997 ed.

[3]   Our provisional preference is for a minimum of three years: see para 5.29 above.

[4]   D A Thomas (1999 ed), cited in this appendix as "Thomas".

[5]   The category is put in interrogative form: "Is it so serious that only custody is appropriate?"

indecent assault; possession of a bladed instrument; possession of an offensive weapon; theft in breach of trust; violent disorder; unlawful wounding or grievous bodily harm; and driving while disqualified.

C.6 The starting point for the following offences is a community penalty, so that, where there are significant aggravating features, it is possible that the defendant would be sentenced to a term of imprisonment. General aggravating factors include the fact that the offence was committed while the defendant was on bail for another offence, or the fact that the defendant has previous convictions and has failed to respond to previous sentences. Examples of offence-related aggravating features are given in brackets.

- non-domestic burglary (aggravating features include racial motivation; deliberately frightening the occupants; that the offence was committed by a group, or at night, or was a professional operation, or involved forcible entry)

- simple possession of a class A drug

- common assault (racial motivation; group action; offender in position of authority; premeditation; use of a weapon; vulnerable victim; victim a public servant)

- going equipped for theft (premeditated; sophisticated equipment; put people in fear)

- handling stolen goods (adult defendant involving children; high value; defendant organiser or distributor)

- obtaining property by deception (committed over lengthy period; high value; two or more defendants involved; vulnerable victim)

- making a false representation to obtain a social security benefit (long period; large amount; organised group; planned deception)

- taking a vehicle without consent (group action; premeditated; related damage; professional; vulnerable victim)

- threatening behaviour (group action; people put in fear; vulnerable victims)

- vehicle interference (group action; planned; related damage)

- dangerous driving (avoiding detection or apprehension; racing; disregard for warnings; excessive speed; prolonged bad driving; serious risk).

C.7 There is a sliding scale for driving with excess alcohol. The legal limit is 35 microgrammes of alcohol per 100 millilitres of breath. Where the offender has over 85 microgrammes per 100 millilitres of breath, the magistrates will consider a community penalty. Aggravating features include the fact that there was a police chase; that injury, fear or damage was caused; that the vehicle was a taxi, bus or heavy goods vehicle; and that the nature of the driving was bad. Above 115 microgrammes, the magistrates will consider custody.

Homicide[6]

C.8 **Drinkald.**[7] D pleaded guilty to attempted murder, having attacked his ex-wife with an axe after a meeting relating to contact with their child, causing her serious injuries. He was suffering from intense depression at the time. A sentence of eight years' imprisonment was reduced to six years on appeal.

C.9 **Mason.**[8] D pleaded guilty to soliciting to murder. He took out a life insurance policy on his wife's life and shortly after separated from her. He offered another man £7,000 to kill her, and supplied him with (mostly useless) weapons. Eight years' imprisonment was reduced to six years on appeal.

C.10 **Wright.**[9] D was convicted of manslaughter by reason of provocation, having been charged with murder. Following his acquittal of an offence of gross indecency with a child, D and his family were subject to abuse and harassment. V broke a window of D's house. D chased him and hit him twice with a pick-axe handle. His sentence of seven years' imprisonment was reduced on appeal to five years.

C.11 **Adamthwaite.**[10] D pleaded guilty to soliciting to murder. He offered to pay an undercover policeman £5,000 to kill his wife, who had formed a relationship with another man. A sentence of six years' imprisonment was reduced to four on appeal.

C.12 **Nixon.**[11] D was convicted of attempted murder and unlawful wounding. He stabbed his wife with a kitchen knife, causing wounds to her cheeks, chest and hands. His sentence of six years was reduced to four on appeal (had the wife died, he would have made out a defence of diminished responsibility on a murder charge).

C.13 **Attorney-General's Reference No 43 of 1996.**[12] D was convicted on two counts of soliciting to murder. She offered an undercover policeman £8,000 to kill a judgment creditor who had indicated that he would sue her for a greater sum. Two years' imprisonment, suspended, was increased to four years on a reference from the Attorney-General.

C.14 **Phillips.**[13] D attacked a man with whom he had been drinking, punching him a number of times. The victim fell and hit his head on the pavement, as a result of

---

[6] Other than causing death by dangerous driving, for which see para C.16 below.

[7] (1988) 10 Cr App R (S) 380 (Thomas B2–13A06).

[8] (1989) 11 Cr App R (S) 74 (Thomas B2–13B04).

[9] (1995) 16 Cr App R (S) 877 (Thomas B1–23B07).

[10] (1993) 15 Cr App R (S) 241 (Thomas B2–13B06).

[11] (1993) 15 Cr App R (S) 429 (Thomas B2–13A15).

[12] [1997] 1 Cr App R (S) 378 (Thomas B2–13B09).

[13] (1985) 7 Cr App R (S) 235 (Thomas B1–33A02).

which he died. A sentence of seven years' imprisonment was reduced on appeal to two years.

C.15   *Kite.*[14] D was convicted of manslaughter. He was the manager of a company which organised leisure activities for children. As a result of failure to maintain proper safety standards, four children were killed when canoeing in the open sea. His sentence of three years' imprisonment was reduced on appeal to two years.

Causing death by dangerous driving

C.16   **Guidelines:** *Boswell.*[15] Drivers who race on the highway, and/or drive with reckless disregard for the safety of others after taking alcohol, may be imprisoned for two years or more.

C.17   *Bevan.*[16] D dangerously overtook a car on a single carriageway road and collided with one car, then a second, killing the driver of the second. His sentence of 18 months' imprisonment was upheld on appeal.

Assaults[17]

C.18   *Attorney-General's References Nos 29, 30 and 31 of 1994 (R v Ribbans, Duggan and Ridley).*[18] The respondents pleaded guilty to causing grievous bodily harm with intent. They attacked V at a garage, knocking him to the ground, punching and kicking him and stabbing him with a screwdriver. One then drove their van over V's legs. The motive was racial, V being a black man whom the respondents had seen with his white girl friend. Sentences of five years (for the respondent who drove the van over V's legs) and three years were increased to seven years and five.

C.19   *McDonagh.*[19] D pleaded guilty to two counts of wounding with intent to cause grievous bodily harm. He attacked his sister and her partner with a machete, almost severing a hand of each (the hands were sewed back into place in hospital). A sentence of six years' imprisonment was reduced to five years on appeal.

C.20   *Ronaldson.*[20] D was convicted of causing grievous bodily harm with intent. He "glassed" (struck in the face with a glass) another in a night-club. The victim suffered six lacerations requiring 17 stitches. The sentence of five years' imprisonment was upheld on appeal.

---

[14]   [1996] 2 Cr App R (S) 295 (Thomas B1–33G08).

[15]   (1984) 79 Cr App R 277.

[16]   [1996] 1 Cr App R (S) 114 (Thomas B1–73D18).

[17]   Other than sexual assaults, for which see para C.29 below.

[18]   (1994) 16 Cr App R (S) 698 (Thomas B2–23I01).

[19]   [1998] 2 Cr App R (S) 195 (Thomas B2–23A21).

[20]   (1990) 12 Cr App R (S) 91 (Thomas B2–23B02).

C.21 **Attorney-General's Reference No 7 of 1994 (R v Chadwick).**[21] D was convicted of assault occasioning actual bodily harm and wounding with intent to cause grievous bodily harm. He punched V, a stranger to him, after V refused to give him some of the food he was eating. Two weeks later, D attacked V as he was leaving a club. During the course of the fight, D, with deliberation, bit off V's thumb from the last joint, and tried to bite him elsewhere on his face. On the hearing of the reference, Taylor CJ referred to D as "bit[ing] another person's face persistently". His sentence of a total of two years' imprisonment was increased to four years, the court stating that, at first instance, the appropriate sentence would have been five years.

C.22 **Gibson.**[22] D was convicted of causing grievous bodily harm with intent. The man with whom a woman D knew lived told him to leave the woman's house. D knocked the man to the ground and kicked his head and face. He sustained a fracture of the eye socket and cheek bone requiring surgery. A sentence of six years' imprisonment was reduced to four and a half on appeal.

C.23 **Moore.**[23] D was convicted of inflicting grievous bodily harm. He had an argument with V about the use of a telephone box. He kicked V about the head and body while he was unconscious. V sustained various facial injuries and was detained in hospital for 17 days. A sentence of three years' imprisonment was upheld on appeal.

C.24 **Broady.**[24] D pleaded guilty to two counts of inflicting grievous bodily harm on his son, when the baby was aged between one and four months. The injuries included fractures of the radius and ulna, a rib and tibia. They had been inflicted on about four occasions. A sentence of three years' imprisonment was upheld on appeal.

C.25 **McLoughlin.**[25] D pleaded guilty to unlawful wounding (a plea of not guilty to wounding with intent was accepted). He struck another in the face with an unbroken glass in a public house. The sentence of three years' imprisonment was reduced to two years on appeal.

C.26 **Rankin and Irvine.**[26] The appellants attacked a mini-cab driver when drunk. V was head-butted, punched and kicked. The attack was accompanied by racist abuse. The appellants were serving police officers. Their sentences of two years' imprisonment were upheld on appeal.

C.27 **Young-Husband.**[27] D pleaded guilty to threatening to kill and to possessing a firearm while committing an offence (assault). He pulled his wife by the hair from

---

[21] (1994) 16 Cr App R (S) 300 (Thomas B2–23C12).

[22] [1997] 1 Cr App R (S) 182 (Thomas B2–23C17).

[23] (1997) 13 Cr App R (S) 130 (Thomas B2–33A05).

[24] (1988) 10 Cr App R (S) 323 (Thomas B2–73B04).

[25] (1985) 7 Cr App R (S) 67 (Thomas B2–33B01).

[26] (1993) 14 Cr App R (S) 636 (Thomas B2–43A06).

[27] (1988) 10 Cr App R (S) 294 (Thomas B2–13D08).

one room to another, put a knife to her throat and threatened to kill her. He then loaded his shotgun and twice pointed it at her before firing past her. A sentence of three years' imprisonment was reduced to 18 months on appeal.

C.28 **Greenhill.**[28] D pleaded guilty to inflicting grievous bodily harm. She lost her temper with her four-week old son, who was crying, and threw him towards his crib. She then hit him on the head about six times. He sustained fractures of the skull and lower leg. Her sentence of three years' imprisonment was reduced on appeal to 12 months.

Sexual offences

C.29 **Guidelines for rape: Billam.**[29] "For rape committed by an adult without any aggravating or mitigating features, a figure of five years should be taken as the starting point in a contested case. Where a rape is committed by two or more men acting together, or by a man who has broken into or otherwise gained access to a place where the victim is living, or by a person who is in a position of responsibility towards the victim, or by a person who abducts the victim and holds her captive, the starting point should be eight years. At the top of the scale comes the defendant who has carried out what might be described as a campaign of rape ... . He represents a more than ordinary danger and a sentence of 15 years or more may be appropriate." Aggravating features include the use of excess violence, the use of a weapon, repeated rape, careful planning, relevant previous convictions, further sexual indignities or perversions, a very old or a very young victim, and any effects of special seriousness on the victim.

C.30 **Attorney-General's Reference No 2 of 1992 (R v Bailey).**[30] D pleaded guilty to aggravated burglary and rape. At night and masked, he entered a bungalow occupied by three young women. He took one of the women into a bedroom at knife-point, raped her twice and forced her to perform oral sex. He was found to be in possession of photographs of the occupants stolen before the rape. The total sentence was increased from six years' imprisonment to eight years.

C.31 **Evans.**[31] D pleaded guilty to seven counts of indecent assault. Over a period of three years, he indecently assaulted his adopted daughter (from the age of 12) by, inter alia, digital penetration of her vagina and oral sex. He obtained her silence by threats of violence or being sent back into care. He was caught assaulting her by his wife. His sentence of eight years' imprisonment was reduced on appeal to six years.

C.32 **Attorney-General's Reference No 35 of 1992 (R v Taylor).**[32] D was convicted of rape. He grabbed a 16-year-old girl and pushed her onto the ground in an alley.

---

[28]   (1986) 8 Cr App R (S) 261 (Thomas B2–73A03).

[29]   (1986) 8 Cr App R (S) 48 (Thomas B4–12002).

[30]   (1992) 14 Cr App R (S) 187 (Thomas B4–13B09).

[31]   (1988) 10 Cr App R (S) 308 (Thomas B4–63A17).

[32]   (1993) 15 Cr App R (S) 233 (Thomas B4–13F11).

There he partially undressed her, forced his penis into her mouth and raped her. His sentence of four years' imprisonment was increased to six years.

C.33   *Pilgrim*.[33] D was convicted of indecent assault. He accosted a 15-year-old girl, forced her to take his penis in her mouth and ejaculated. His sentence of five years' imprisonment was reduced to three years on appeal.

C.34   *Hessey*.[34] D pleaded guilty to three counts of indecent assault. On a number of occasions over a period of 12 months, he fingered the vagina of the 12-year-old daughter of the woman with whom he was living. His sentence of two years' imprisonment was reduced to 15 months on appeal.

Robbery

C.35   *Attorney-General's Reference No 36 of 1992 (R v Hills)*.[35] D pleaded guilty to robbery. With another, he held up five employees at market premises. They were armed with an imitation firearm, a knife and a stake, and stole £5,700. His sentence of three years' imprisonment was increased to five years. Seven years might have been appropriate at first instance.

C.36   *Gee*.[36] D pleaded guilty to robbery. He threw petrol over a garage attendant, produced a box of matches and demanded money. He took £50. His sentence of five years' imprisonment was upheld on appeal.

C.37   *Hearne*.[37] D pleaded guilty to robbery. He gained access to the home of a 90-year-old woman whom he knew. He pushed her onto a bed, tied a jumper over her face and took a purse containing £30. His sentence of five years' imprisonment was reduced on appeal to three years.

C.38   *Attorney-General's Reference No 26 of 1992 (R v Green)*.[38] D pleaded guilty to robbery, handling and threatening behaviour. He approached three men in a stationary car, threatened one with a knife and demanded rings and a wrist watch. Earlier, he had received stolen property obtained in a similar robbery, and threatened one of the victims who rejected his offer of returning the property in exchange for a car radio. His sentence of 18 months' imprisonment, suspended, was increased to two and a half years.

Theft and fraud

C.39   **Guidelines on theft[39] by person in position of trust: *Clark*.[40]** The guidelines relate to defendants "in a position of trust, for example, an accountant, solicitor,

---

[33]   (1992) 14 Cr App R (S) 432 (Thomas B4–63C22).

[34]   (1987) 9 Cr App R (S) 268 (Thomas B4–63A10).

[35]   (1993) 15 Cr App R (S) 117 (Thomas B6–23B29).

[36]   (1990) 12 Cr App R (S) 268 (Thomas B6–23B18).

[37]   [1998] 1 Cr App R (S) 333 (Thomas B6–23C14).

[38]   (1993) 15 Cr App R (S) 61 (Thomas B6–23D12).

[39]   In practice, these guidelines are also applied to similar offences.

[40]   [1998] 2 Cr App R (S) 95 (Thomas B6–12003), updating *Barrick* (1985) 7 Cr App R (S) 142 (Thomas B6–12002).

bank employee or postman" who has used his or her position "to defraud his partners or clients or employers or the general public".[41] "Where the amount is not small, but is less than £17,500, terms of imprisonment from the very short up to 21 months will be appropriate; cases involving sums between £17,500 and £100,000 will merit two to three years; cases involving sums between £100,000 and £250,000 will merit three to four years; cases involving between £250,000 and £1 million will merit between five and nine years; cases involving £1 million or more will merit ten years or more. These terms are appropriate for contested cases."

C.40 **Guidelines on benefit fraud: Stewart.**[42] At the top of the range, requiring substantial sentences (perhaps of two and a half years' imprisonment and upwards), are carefully organised frauds on a large scale, in which considerable sums of money are obtained, often by means of frequent changes of name and address or forged or stolen documents. The length of the custodial sentence will depend in the first instance on the scope of the fraud.

C.41 **Shaw.**[43] D pleaded guilty to four counts of theft and asked for a further 15 to be taken into consideration. He was a solicitor. Over about seven years he stole about £3 million, £1 million for his own use and the remainder to conceal the earlier offences. He had admitted the offences on his own initiative. The sentence of seven years' imprisonment was reduced to six years on appeal.

C.42 **de Beer.**[44] D pleaded guilty to various counts of obtaining property and services by deception and obtaining credit as an undischarged bankrupt. He fraudulently obtained commercial lease agreements relating to apparently non-existent machinery and obtained loans to purchase equipment to lease, the companies involved all being owned by him. Over about five years, he obtained £1.3 million. He also fraudulently applied for a mortgage on a property and fraudulently obtained a credit card. The amount lost was over £500,000. The total sentence of six years' imprisonment was reduced to five years on appeal.

C.43 **Nall-Cain (Lord Brocket).**[45] D pleaded guilty to conspiracy to defraud and obtaining by deception. He insured a number of classic cars for £4.5 million (£1.5 million over their real value), then persuaded two employees to stage a fake burglary and destroy the cars. The insurance company refused to pay, but lost about £200,000 as a result of the terms of the settlement of an action taken against it by D. His sentence of five years' imprisonment was upheld on appeal.

[41] *Barrick* (1985) 7 Cr App R (S) 142.

[42] (1989) 11 Cr App R (S) 132 (Thomas F3–2A12).

[43] [1996] 2 Cr App R (S) 278 (Thomas B6–13D17).

[44] [1997] 1 Cr App R (S) 97 (Thomas B6–33E14).

[45] [1998] 2 Cr App R (S) 145 (Thomas B6–33C15).

C.44 **D'Souza.**[46] D pleaded guilty to theft. A bookkeeper to a teaching hospital, he stole £652,000 over about ten years. The sentence of five years' imprisonment was reduced to four years on appeal.

C.45 **Mangham.**[47] D pleaded guilty to using a false instrument with intent and obtaining a money transfer by deception. A care worker, he obtained possession of a pass book belonging to a 95-year-old woman in his charge and forged her signature on two occasions, obtaining £5,000. His sentence of two years' imprisonment was reduced on appeal to 18 months.

Burglary

C.46 **Betts.**[48] D pleaded guilty to burglary. He forced the door of a house while the occupiers were absent and stole electrical goods worth £410. His sentence of three years' imprisonment was reduced on appeal to 21 months.

Handling stolen goods

C.47 **Amlani and Smith.**[49] D2 had received a quantity of stolen mobile telephones, and D1 made arrangements for their sale. Their sentences of 30 months' imprisonment were reduced on appeal to 21 months.

Arson

C.48 **Gannon.**[50] D pleaded guilty to arson, being reckless as to whether life was endangered, on the basis that he started the fire accidentally but then made no effort to put it out. The fire was in the loft of a block of houses. Four people were in the premises at the time, and substantial damage was caused. His sentence of five years' imprisonment was reduced on appeal to three and a half years.

Perverting the course of justice

C.49 **Riley.**[51] D pleaded guilty to making statements tending to pervert the course of justice. His nephew was awaiting trial for rape. D approached the complainant, suggested that she should not give evidence, and made an implied threat of violence. His sentence of three years' imprisonment was reduced to 15 months on appeal.

Corruption

C.50 **Wilson.**[52] D was convicted of conspiracy to commit corruption and three counts of corruption. A buyer with a large manufacturing concern, he accepted

---

[46] [1996] 2 Cr App R (S) 130 (Thomas B6–13D16).

[47] [1998] 2 Cr App R (S) 344 (Thomas B6–13A17).

[48] (1990) 12 Cr App R (S) 457 (Thomas B6–43A04).

[49] (1994) 16 Cr App R (S) 339 (Thomas B6–53A06).

[50] (1990) 12 Cr App R (S) 545 (Thomas B7–13B07).

[51] (1990) 12 Cr App R (S) 410 (Thomas B8–23A07).

[52] (1982) 4 Cr App R (S) 33 (Thomas B9–13A02).

consideration worth £2,500 in return for showing favour to a supplier to his employer. His sentence of three and a half years' imprisonment was reduced on appeal to 18 months.

Drug offences

C.51 **Olumide.**[53] D pleaded guilty to fraudulently importing 140.9 grammes of heroin. The drug was concealed in his anus when he entered the UK at an airport. His sentence of seven years' imprisonment was upheld on appeal.

C.52 **Netts.**[54] D was convicted of possessing cannabis with intent to supply. He was stopped in his car, which contained 90 kilograms of cannabis resin. He was sentenced as a courier. His sentence of seven years' imprisonment was reduced on appeal to five years.

C.53 **Howard.**[55] D pleaded guilty to four counts of supplying crack cocaine. He was a retail supplier. His sentence of five years' imprisonment was reduced on appeal to four years.

C.54 **Blyth.**[56] D pleaded guilty to being knowingly concerned in the fraudulent evasion of the prohibition on the importation of cannabis resin. He was found in possession of 16 kilograms of the drug. He admitted to having made three previous trips to import cannabis. His sentence of two years was upheld on appeal.

---

[53] (1987) 9 Cr App R (S) 364 (Thomas B11–23A02).

[54] [1997] 2 Cr App R (S) 117 (Thomas B11–13C07).

[55] [1996] 2 Cr App R (S) 273 (Thomas B11–23E06).

[56] [1996] 1 Cr App R (S) 388 (Thomas B11–13A10).